Designing for Growth

Designing for Growth:
a design thinking tool kit for managers

By Jeanne Liedtka and Tim Ogilvie

Columbia Business School
Publishing

Columbia University Press
Publishers Since 1893
New York   Chichester, West Sussex
Copyright © 2011 Columbia University Press
All rights reserved

Library of Congress Cataloging-in-Publication Data

Liedtka, Jeanne.
    Designing for growth : a design thinking tool kit for managers / by Jeanne Liedtka and Tim Ogilvie.
      p. cm.
    Includes bibliographical references.
    ISBN 978-0-231-15838-1 (cloth : alk. paper) — ISBN 978-0-231-52796-5 (ebook)
  1. Creative ability in business. 2. Organizational change. 3. Success in business. I. Ogilvie, Tim. II. Title.
    HD53.L543 2011
    658.4′063—dc22

                                      2010053277

References to Internet Web sites (URLs) were accurate at the time of writing. Neither the authors nor Columbia University Press is responsible for URLs that may have expired or changed since the manuscript was prepared.

To Salz and Caroline

ACKNOWLEDGEMENTS

We both owe much to the Darden School of Business at the University of Virginia and the Batten Institute and their leadership. They brought us together and supported us every step of the way. We are especially grateful to Dean Robert Bruner and Batten Institute Managing Director Elizabeth O'Halloran, each of whom helped Jeanne find the time and then Jeanne and Tim the resources to accomplish this project. And to David Newkirk, who continued to tell us that our efforts would matter to managers.

And then there is our trusted editor, Amy Halliday. Amy has the gift of knowing when to push and when to pull. We are grateful for her unfailing candor, patience, and generous advice. She was a relentless advocate for the practicing manager. If this book does not appeal to the sensibilities of managers, it is not for lack of effort by her.

The other crucial member of our team comes from Tim's good deeds. Eight years ago, he cofounded an innovation strategy consulting firm, and Jenny Lynn Cargiuolo joined that firm. Her first job; Peer Insight's first designer. Today we think of her as a design Yoda, and every key design concept in this book was vetted by her. Admittedly, several over-simplifications in the book exist over her staunch objections (or what Jenny charmingly refers to as her "dead body").

Myles Thompson and Bridget Flannery-McCoy at Columbia University Press shepherded us through the publication process with effortless wisdom and constant cheer—even when Tim managed to lose the signed contracts in the mail. (Sorry, Bridget. But it all worked out, didn't it?) The gorgeous layout of the book is the work of visual genius Daniel Lombardi. The early drafts were shaped by Preethi Lakshminarayanan.

From Jeanne

I want to begin by thanking Tim, my coauthor. I look at the finished product that our partnership has wrought, compare it to my text-laden, unimaginatively illustrated previous writing efforts, and thank my lucky stars for the coincidence that brought Tim to the Darden School. To think, as I did when I initially began this project, that I could do justice to the world of design thinking without a partner who lived and breathed design was utterly foolhardy. But Tim brought so much more to this effort than his extraordinary talent for visualization—he brought stories, tools, unfailing good humor, intelligence, and persistence. Most important, he brought such an innate talent for demonstrating design thinking every step of the way that it was impossible to lose sight of our topic—and why it so enriches traditional business thinking. This book is a living embodiment, for me, of what happens when design and business come together.

I also want to thank my Darden colleagues and friends, who have made the school a very special home for me for two decades now, creating a place I find it unimaginable not to be part of. It seems to me that almost everything I know that feels important was learned from one of you. And my fascination with exploring where humanity and business intersect can surely be traced to four culprits: Ed Freeman, Alec Horniman, and Jack and Carol Weber. This fearsome foursome are my Yodas.

Karen Musselman makes my life at Darden wonderful by bringing the force of her wisdom and orderliness to tame my chaos. Andrew King never fails to answer my distress call. Ed Hess has been a source of inspiration and encouragement, and I consider luring him to Darden my greatest gift to the school. Lynn Isabella and Susan Chaplinsky have made becoming an MFL actually fun. And, finally, thanks to all the Darden students who struggled to learn this stuff along with me and taught me as much as I taught them.

Then there is the wonderful group of thought leaders who took me by the hand and patiently educated this most traditional of strategists about design: Roger Martin (for leading the way), Angela Meyer (for never once suggesting that I was in way over my head), and Nathan Shedroff, Heather Fraser, and Maureen Thurston (for taking me from crayons to perfume).

On a personal note, I have my large and wonderful family (who keep me humble) and old and dear friends (who keep me sane) to thank. To my sister Jane, especially, who has been the most constant source of support and encouragement in my life for the past thirty-odd years (Rehoboth aside).

Finally, to Salz, the most courageous and creative thinker I've ever met. Thank you, Taco Bell!

From Tim

Writing a book is a preposterous idea to a busy consultant who moonlights as a husband, father, and neglectful friend. I can't contemplate making any acknowledgements without first acknowledging my coauthor, Jeanne Liedtka. If you know Jeanne, then you know the term "force of nature" is not hyperbole. Her incendiary intellect is perfectly balanced by an utter lack of pretension and a relentless energy to get it done. The approachable authorial voice of the book is Jeanne's. I just learned to mimic it. And the generous spirit of encouragement? That's all her—she just puts it out there, as naturally as breathing.

It occurs to me that writing a book and working seem incompatible. Someone had to mind the store. My business partner Gordon Hui did more than that. When Jeanne invited me to the project, I hesitated. Gordon insisted that I accept. A few months into the project, my father fell ill. I decided to drop out; it was only fair to Jeanne and Amy. "Absolutely not," he advised. My father recovered, and so did the book.

Jeneanne Rae, my other business partner and cofounder of our firm, did not bear the same burden of prodding me. She just had to keep the business afloat. During a global recession. Nearly a decade ago, Jeneanne uttered, in a *Graduate*-style aside, her advice for my future: service innovation. Little did she know I would embrace her advice—and her—so wholeheartedly.

Many other members of our firm chipped in, mostly by teaching me lessons on their projects but also by providing a key story, reading early chapters, and digging up obscure facts and sources. These contributors include Katie Waterson, Kimberly Campbell, Carl Fudge, Pat Dewey, Jamie Mash, Colin Hudson, and Kristin Metropolous.

How did I learn what I wrote about? It was on the backs of a short list of courageous clients over the past eight years who shared their hopes and challenges and invited me to partner with them. In less than a decade, I went from wide-eyed adventurer to aspiring sage. The clients that have aided in this conversion include Mark Hadding at Siemens, Diane Ty and Rick Bowers at AARP, Jacqueline LeSage Krause and Dave Peak at The Hartford, Iain Campbell and Bob Russell at York, Claudia Kotchka and Cindy Tripp at P&G, Dave Jarrett and Steve Josey at Crowe Horwath, Dale McIntyre at Behr, Melody Roberts and Denis Weil at McDonald's, Lem Lasher at CSC, Sam Lucente, Debbie Mrazek, and Glenna Patton at Hewlett-Packard, Lauri Kien Kotcher at Godiva (formerly at Pfizer), Peter Westerstrahle and Tiina Tanninen-Ahonen at Tekes, Scott Williams at Starwood Hotels, Austin Henderson at Pitney Bowes, Kirby McDaniel at Hallmark, and Andy Winslow at Celestica. These are people of uncommon courage and generosity. I am deeply in their debt.

The cool thing about the innovation field is that everybody talks to one another (unlike strategy consulting, the world I came from). I must acknowledge a small group of professional collaborators who shared their wisdom along the way. In deference to brevity, the list starts with Larry Keeley at Doblin and Mike Nuttall, cofounder of IDEO. I learned a lot at their respective knees. After that, I was shepherded by Dev Patnaik at Jump, Scott Stropkay and Bill Hartman at Essential, Shelley Evenson of CMU (and now Microsoft), and Stan Gryskiewicz at the Association of Innovation Managers. Stan is one of the most gifted mentors one will ever meet.

In addition to mentors, one needs inspiration to stick with a challenging project. Carter Griffin convinced me that writing a book is a perfectly reasonable thing to do. And his contributions go deeper: Just over a decade ago, Carter taught me how to collaborate. Similarly inspiring was Mark Stein (whom you will meet in the context of Brivo Systems, featured in Section III). Mark is one of the most amazing, talented, daring, and caring people I can imagine. Court Ogilvie helped me re-energize during runs along the Potomac and generously offered editorial advice. My climbing partner of 25 years—and brother for a bit longer—was a constant source of laughter and inspiration.

If you recall, I mention that I moonlight as a husband? Well, the woman upon whom that pale light occasionally falls, Caroline Altmann, is the quintessential hybrid thinker: a Columbia MBA who has had a solo show of her art. When I took on this project, she understood the 1000-to-1 ratio of effort to finished product, which was an abstraction to me. Artist-Caroline was always there to nurture my inner design thinker, helping to explore new solutions to an awkward section. MBA-Caroline would then offer insightful criticism. By reflecting against her expansive, whole-minded energy, I saw our topic of design thinking as a world of infinite possibility. I hope those possibilities shine through in this book.

Jeanne Liedtka and Tim Ogilvie
Charlottesville and Alexandria, VA
December 2010

SECTION I:

The Why and How of Design Thinking

CHAPTER ONE:
WHY DESIGN?

Every manager needs design. You can't grow a business without it. But what is it? Asked to describe design, Tim Brennan of Apple's Creative Services group drew the following picture:[1]

Design, this clever definition asserts, is simply magic. It is an utter enigma, a mysterious no-man's-land where only the brave (and the brilliant) dare tread. It mocks any idea that a formal process could exist for navigating those many hairpin turns. Sure—we'd all like to discover the equivalent of the iPod in our own businesses. But mere mortals—especially business types—are out of their league when it comes to unleashing that kind of innovation and growth. And so we throw up our hands and go back to poring over spreadsheets and market research reports in our search for the next silver bullet, the next catalyst for growth.

But don't be put off by Apple's view of design. Design has a lot of different meanings. And it turns out that the design thinking process that we are going to talk about in this book is more akin to Dorothy's ruby slippers than a magic wand. You've already got the power. You just need to figure out how to use it. Find a leader of innovation in any organization, and he or she has likely been practicing design thinking all along.

If you are a manager reading this book, get ready to roll up your sleeves—not throw up your hands. Because design thinking is actually a systematic approach to problem solving. It starts with customers and the ability to create a better future for them. It acknowledges that we probably won't get that right the first time. It does not require supernatural powers. This kind of design is absolutely safe to try at home.

And design's time has come.

We believe that the recent explosion of interest in design thinking has a lot more fueling it than Apple's success and high profile. We are looking for a new tool kit. We've come to the end of the runway on maximizing productivity and re-engineering processes. Competition has upped the ante: The Internet and the arrival of networking have made knowledge impossible to hoard. Our views of where creativity comes from are expanding: We are learning new things about our brain every day and recognizing different cognitive modes and how they perform in different contexts. Finally, the tools of design—including Post-it notes and whiteboards—have become simple and ubiquitous.

DAVE JARRETT

Think hotbed of design thinking. Think CPAs and tax accountants. Are you confused yet?

The first time you talk to Dave Jarrett, a partner at Crowe Horwath, one of the largest accounting firms in the United States, he just might ask if you've heard the joke about how you become a partner in a CPA firm. "You never get a better offer," he deadpans.

Dave joined Crowe in 1975 and spent two decades as an auditor and tax expert. For the past ten years, he has headed up a group that helps develop solutions aimed at enhancing the firm's capabilities, market recognition, sales, and profitability. And he knows how you feel.

DESIGN THINKER

> "Design thinking intimidates people—it almost feels like it's a different skill set than what us normal people can do. When you think of design, your mind immediately goes to fashion, and I can't even pick out two things that should be worn at the same time. But what we're really trying to do here is make sure we're building something the way a buyer would like to have it."

Design thinking can do for organic growth and innovation what TQM did for quality—take something we always have cared about and put tools and processes into the hands of managers to make it happen.

Whether design thinking can—or should—be taught to managers is a hotly debated topic among designers. How you define design itself lies at the core of the argument. Designers bristle at the suggestion that managers can be taught enough about design to be anything but dangerous. They point to the years of specialized training that designers receive—and worry that unleashing managers to think of themselves as designers will erode the quality of and appreciation for what trained designers do. We believe that their concerns need to be taken seriously and that the way to do this is to differentiate *design* from *design thinking*.

Gifted designers combine an aesthetic sensibility with deep capabilities for visualization, ethnography, and pattern recognition that are well beyond the grasp of most of us—managers included. But when it comes to fostering business growth, the talent that we are interested in is not rooted in either natural gifts or studio training—it lies with having a systematic approach to problem solving. That, to us, defines design thinking, and it can be taught to managers.

Like any process, design thinking will be practiced at varying levels by people with different talents and capabilities. Can your average manager be transformed into Jonathan Ive, Apple's chief designer? No more than your local tennis pro can turn you into Serena Williams. But can you improve your game? Absolutely. And having done that, we can guarantee that your appreciation for what the Jonathan Ives of the world do will have grown rather than diminished. More important, you will have a new tool kit to approach your growth challenge.

This book aims to demystify design thinking by translating "design" from an abstract idea into a practical, everyday tool any manager can profit from. Using a business perspective and business language, we'll translate the vocabulary of design, unpack the mysterious connection between design thinking and profitable growth, introduce a systematic process (complete with simple project management aids), and teach you the ten tools you'll need to marry the design approach to traditional business thinking in ways that enhance your ability to profitably grow your business. In the process, we'll introduce you to more people like Dave Jarrett, none of whom were trained in design, all of whom are using design thinking to drive innovation and growth in their organizations. People like Christi Zuber, a nurse with a passion for design, and Diane Ty, first a poly sci major, then an MBA on a mission at AARP to encourage young adults to make better financial choices—and help baby boomers get their adult kids off the payroll. All of these managers mastered design thinking. So saddle up those ruby slippers and let's get moving.

What if Managers Thought Like Designers?

But let's not get ahead of ourselves. What would be different if managers thought more like designers? We have three words for you: empathy, invention, and iteration.

Design starts with *empathy,* establishing a deep understanding of those we are designing for. Managers who thought like designers would put themselves in their customers' shoes. Of course, we all know already that we are supposed to be "customer-centered," but what we are talking about here is deeper and more personal than that. It means "knowing" customers as real people with real problems, not seeing them as targets for sales or as a set of demographic statistics around age, income level, or marital status. It involves developing an understanding of both their emotional and their "rational" needs and wants. The actor Stephen Fry (the ultimate Jeeves), writing about Apple's latest product after interviewing chief designer Jonathan Ive, noted in an April 2010 issue of *Time:*

> *"Consider for a moment. We are human beings; our first responses are dominated not by cal-culations but by feelings. What Ive and his team understand is that if you have an object in*

your pocket or hand for hours every day, then your relationship with it is profound, human, and emotional."[2]

Great designs inspire—they grab us at an emotional level. One of the saddest facts about the state of business is the extent to which we so often settle for mediocrity. We don't even attempt to engage our customers—or our employees—at an emotional level, let alone inspire them. Yet the difference between great designs and those that are only okay is the way the former call us to something greater.

Consider the difference between the San Francisco Bay Bridge and the Golden Gate Bridge.[3] The Bay Bridge offers a route across the water. The Golden Gate Bridge does that, too, but it also sweeps, symbolizes, and enthralls. It has, like other design icons such as the Sydney Opera House, become a symbol of the land it occupies. How many of our business inventions are that compelling? Too few.

Since design is also a process of *invention,* managers who thought like designers would think of themselves as creators. For all our talk about the "art and science" of management, we have mostly paid attention to the science part. Taking design seriously means acknowledging the difference between what scientists do and what designers and growth leaders do. Whereas scientists investigate today to discover explanations for what already is, designers invent tomorrow—they create something that isn't. To get to growth, we have to create something in the future that is different from the present. But powerful futures are rarely discovered primarily through analytics. They are, as Walt Disney said, "created first in the mind and next in the activity." This doesn't deny analysis an important role, but it does subordinate analysis to the process of invention when the goal is growth.

Great design, it has been said by Richard Buchanan, former Dean of Carnegie Mellon's School of Design, occurs at the intersection of constraint, contingency, and possibility—elements that are central to creating innovative, elegant, and functional designs.[4] But it matters greatly with which of these you start. In business, we have tended to start the growth conversation with constraints: the constraints of budgets, of ease of implementation, of the quarterly earnings focus that Wall Street dictates. As a result, we get designs for tomorrow that merely tweak today. Great design inevitably starts with the question "What if anything were possible?" After all, if growth is about invention and our assumptions about constraints bound what we can imagine, then seeing beyond these is job number one.

Consider the design of one of America's great public spaces: New York's Central Park. In 1857, the country's first public landscape design competition was held to select the plan for this park. Of all the submissions, only one—prepared by Frederick Law Olmsted and Calvert Vaux—fulfilled all of the design requirements. The most challenging—that crosstown vehicular traffic be permitted without marring the pastoral feel of the park—had been considered impossible to solve by all other entrants to the competition. Olmsted and Vaux succeeded by eliminating the assumption that the park was a two-dimensional space. Instead, they imagined the park in three dimensions and sank four roads eight feet below its surface.

Finally, design insists that we prepare ourselves to *iterate* our way to a solution, so managers who thought like designers would see themselves as learners. Most managers are taught a straightforward linear problem-solving methodology: define a problem, identify various solutions, analyze each, and choose one—the right one. Designers aren't nearly so impatient—or optimistic. They understand that successful invention takes experimentation and that empathy is hard won. So the task is one of learning.

Consider IKEA. When the company's visionary founder, Ingvar Kamprad, started out, he had only a general sense of what would become IKEA's revolutionary approach to the furniture business. Nearly every element of IKEA's now legendary business model—showrooms and catalogs in tandem, knockdown furniture in flat parcels, and customer pick-up and assembly—emerged over time from experimental responses to urgent problems. Customer pick-up, for instance, became a central element of IKEA's strategy almost by chance, when frustrated customers rushed into the warehouse because there weren't enough employees to help them. The store manager realized the advantages of the customers' initiative and suggested that the idea become permanent. "Regard every problem as a possibility," was Kamprad's mantra—and so in designing he focused less on control and "getting it right" the first time and more on learning and on seeing and responding to opportunities as they emerged.

A great park, an iconic bridge, an innovative business model—they share fundamental design principles: Don't let your imagined constraints limit your possibilities; aim to connect deeply with those you serve; seek opportunities, not perfection. But design brings more than just a set of principles; it also brings a methodology and a collection of tools that can help us realize those aspirations.

We wrote this book because we each fell in love with the idea of design about a decade ago, coming from very different places: Jeanne after spending most of her life on the business strategy side as a strategy consultant and professor focused on organic growth. Tim as a systems engineer turned entrepreneur turned cofounder of an innovation firm. Neither of us trained as a designer. We like to say that Thomas Jefferson brought us and design together.

Design and Business: A Match Made in Heaven—or Hell?

We believe that the differences between a "traditional" business approach and a "design" approach are profound, yet the two are potentially so complementary that they can form a match made in heaven—or hell. Like opposites that attract—or repel—together they may be magic or misery.

Consider a challenge faced by a leading consumer products firm: how to think about and respond to changes in the retail marketplace over the next ten years. Suppose that two student teams—one composed of MBAs and the other of design students—tackle the issue. How might each team approach its study?

The MBAs would likely begin by researching trends in the marketplace—social, technological, environmental, and political. They'd read analysts' reports, interview industry experts, and benchmark leading retailers and competitors. They'd produce forecasts and a recommended set of strategies, complete with ROI (return on investment) and NPV (net present value) calculations. They'd deliver it all in a PowerPoint presentation.

The design students would probably approach the project quite differently. They might begin with a similar trend analysis, but they would use it to develop scenarios of possible futures

MR. JEFFERSON'S UNIVERSITY

The University of Virginia, Tim's alma mater and Jeanne's academic home for the past twenty years, provided the introduction to design for both of us. And what an introduction it was! Thomas Jefferson was the third President of the United States and author of the Declaration of Independence. He had a passionate, lifelong dedication to public education and devoted the last decade of his life to creating the University of Virginia.

He called it the "hobby of my old age … and the last service that I can render my country." Jefferson himself was personally responsible for every aspect of its design and implementation, from the architecture of its buildings and grounds to the composition of its curriculum and the selection of its faculty. It is impossible to dwell long in his beloved "academical village" and not be touched by how he used the power of design to shape the future.

Like all great designs, UVA starts out with both a challenge and a belief. The challenge—one of great concern to Jefferson and all of the founding fathers—was how to preserve a fragile democracy when the first generation of leaders had passed on. He believed that an educated electorate would make the right choices. For Jefferson, the link between democracy and education was clear—without an educated populace, there was no hope of protecting self-government.

To the modern observer, Jefferson's genius may appear to lie in the beauty of the architecture that he created—but in reality, he took much of his architectural inspiration directly from the sixteenth century Italian architect Palladio. His true genius lay with the power of the space that he created—both physical and mental—and its ability to evoke so vividly the purpose for which it was designed. Jefferson's university was designed to be a community that rejected hierarchy, where faculty and students worked as partners to pursue the kind of learning that democracy required.

The architecture—a series of small buildings arrayed around a common—embodied this ambition. The curriculum would include the new "scientific" and "pragmatic" fields like botany and agriculture, appropriate to a democracy rather than an aristocracy, and student self-government would be the principle upon which the new university would run.

What Jefferson designed was much more than a set of buildings; it was an educational experience—of a very particular kind. All aspects of UVA's design, from the architecture to the curriculum to the selection of faculty and methods of governance, emerge out of an image that Jefferson holds of the educational experience that he committed to creating. An education for democracy. Like all great design, our campus inspires students and faculty alike as it puts us to work.

instead of spreadsheets. They would hang out in stores and talk to shoppers and employees, focusing on the shopping experience. They'd likely create some different customer personas and use the scenarios to try to model the changes in the personas' lives—and, accordingly, in their shopping habits—over the next ten years. They might sponsor a "store of the future" brainstorming session, inviting their fellow students (and offering free pizza). They would use the scenarios and personas as a starting point and build on them as a group. Ultimately, they'd present not solutions but a small number of concepts to be prototyped, with the aim of soliciting feedback from real customers and collaborators.

These obvious differences in framing, data gathering, and output signal more fundamental differences in the core assumptions and decision drivers underlying each approach. Business thinking assumes rationality and objectivity. Its decision driver is cold, clean, economic logic. Reality is precise and quantifiable. There is "truth"—and answers are "right" or "wrong." Design assumes instead human experience, always messy, as its decision driver and sees true objectivity as an illusion. Reality, for designers, is always constructed by the people living it. Decisions in this world are seen as driven by emotion more than logic; desire is seen as a more powerful motivator than reason. In this world, there is only our individual "truth"—and answers are "better" or "worse." Hence, the MBAs analyzed trend data; the designers observed the shopper's experience.

But the asymmetry goes even deeper. Even the very values on which each approach rests diverge dramatically. And this has a lot to do with messiness versus order. As one Procter & Gamble vice president explained to us, "At P&G we like neat, tidy conversations, but we realized early on that embracing design meant we were going to have to get comfortable with messy conversations." Business executives, more often than not, value order and control above all else—and structure their organizations to produce it. "At Abbott our motto is, Plan the work, then work the plan," we recall an Abbott executive telling us. No surprise there—you would, of course, expect this of people who run large organizations and are held accountable for achieving carefully forecasted quarterly performance. Ambiguity and uncertainty make them uncomfortable; they crave predictability. Innovation is just plain messy and often inefficient—there is no way around that. But ambiguity and uncertainty are like crack cocaine to designers. And so the MBAs benchmark competitors to identify what "leading edge" companies are doing today; the designers envision several futuristic worlds to prototype for and play in.

Not surprisingly, these differences in core values and assumptions translate into very different tools and practices—and people who often make each other nervous. Business thinking favors analytical approaches; decision-making processes demand "proof" that we have arrived at the "correct" answer. So the MBAs make their case with ROIs and PowerPoints. Design, in contrast, favors trying over extensive planning and is overwhelmingly experimental in its approach. Designers expect to iterate their way to increasingly "better" answers; so the designers create prototypes with paper, foam core, or video.

Finally, in business we almost always dwell in the land of either the abstract—producing pro formas and corporate visions at 20,000 feet—or the very specific (did you get that order out?). Design, as a practice, iterates not only in time but also across levels. It moves continuously back and forth between levels of abstraction, between the big picture and the concrete—and seeks comfort in the tangible. Designers produce models and prototypes that make ideas feel real, rather than spreadsheets and mission statements that dwell in abstractions. So here is where we end up:

	BUSINESS	DESIGN
Underlying Assumptions	Rationality, objectivity; Reality as fixed and quantifiable	Subjective experience; Reality as socially constructed
Method	Analysis aimed at proving one "best" answer	Experimentation aimed at iterating toward a "better" answer
Process	Planning	Doing
Decision Drivers	Logic; Numeric models	Emotional insight; Experiential models
Values	Pursuit of control and stability; Discomfort with uncertainty	Pursuit of novelty; Dislike of status quo
Levels of Focus	Abstract or particular	Iterative movement between abstract and particular

It seems, then, that business is from Mars and design is from Venus (to borrow an oft-used phrase). So why even try to put them together? Because—like most opposites—they have a lot to offer each other.

You're Not in Kansas Anymore

In today's increasingly fast-paced and unpredictable environment, business needs design precisely because of all the differences we've noted:

First, design is all about action, and business too often gets stuck at the talking stage. Let's face it—despite all our planning and analyzing and controlling, business's track record at translating its rhetoric into results is not impressive. The academics who study these things estimate that only somewhere between 10 percent and 60 percent of the promised returns of new strategies are actually delivered.[5] Not much of a performance, even at the high end of the estimates. Practices that consume enormous amounts of our time and attention—like writing mission statements—produce discouraging results. One recent global study found that an impressive 82 percent of the 300-plus firms surveyed had mission statements. Unfortunately, less than half the managers interviewed thought that those statements had anything to do with the reality of their day-to-day business.[6]

JEREMY ALEXIS, DESIGNER AND PROFESSOR

Illinois Institute of Technology

" When people ask me what design thinking is, I always go back to Gregory Treverton, a policy analyst at the Rand Corporation, who noted, 'There are two types of problems. There are mysteries and there are puzzles. Puzzles are problems where when you have the right level of data disclosure, when you have that absolute number, the problem can be solved.' In his example, it's finding Osama Bin Laden—if we had GPS coordinates, we'd know where he is.

There's another category of problem called mysteries, where there is no single piece of data, there is no level of data disclosure that will actually solve a problem. In fact, there might be too much data and it's about interpreting all the data that's there. And that's a richer, harder problem that requires more systems thinking, that requires prototyping and piloting. That's really where the designers are often most adept. Treverton's example here is rebuilding Iraq: There's no single piece of data that will make this task any easier. It's just about trying different things and experimenting and trying to move forward toward a solution … We'll never have enough information. We'll never have the right information. We just have to interpret what we have now and do the best that we can. It's the mysteries that get designers excited.

Too often in the corporate world there's the belief that we can use these PowerPoint reports and charts and statisti-cally significant surveys to generate ideas. That may work for incremental improvements, but if you want something more disruptive you have to go into the field and find something proprietary and experience it for yourself. The old joke is that a lawyer will not ask you a question that he or she does not already know the answer to. It's just the opposite for designers. We ask questions only if we really have no idea: We want to be sponges and soak up ideas from the people we're working with. Inefficiency and ambiguity are both conditions of the design process. There has to be time for reflection and disagreement. These are core to great, new, big ideas. And they are also what makes processes inefficient. It's important to have time within your process to take a step back and look at what you created and consider the connections you're not seeing. You also need time for disagreement because good design thinking is about bringing together a diverse set of inputs.

If you want efficiency, you get everybody who thinks the same way and they'll get to a decision quickly. And that works 80 percent of the time. But for that 20 percent of the time when you need something disruptive, innovative, and creative, you're going to have to put up with a little bit more ambiguity."

All of this empty talk is making it harder and harder to get anything to actually happen—especially in big organizations. We tell managers to be "customer centered" but cut their travel budgets. We ask them to take risks and then punish them for mistakes. And we give them ambitious growth goals and only Excel spreadsheets to achieve them. Reality doesn't work that way. Getting new results requires new tools—and design has real tools to help us move from talk to action.

Second, design teaches us how to make things feel real, and most business rhetoric today remains largely irrelevant to the people who are supposed to make things happen. Executives can buy and sell, they can hire talent, they can talk to Wall Street—but they can't change an organization without a lot of help. The only people who will care enough to help are those for whom the strategy is real. Things that feel real to people, as psychologist William James pointed out over a century ago, are both interesting and personally significant. They are *experienced*, not just pronounced. While managers are showing spreadsheets—the ultimate abstraction—designers are telling stories. We have a lot to learn from design about how to tell a story that engages an audience, captures the experience dimension, and makes the future feel real. Look at any presentation created by anybody at a design firm and compare it with the PowerPoint dreck you are forced to sit through every day at work. Enough said.

Third, design is tailored to dealing with uncertainty, and business's obsession with analysis is best suited for a stable and predictable world. That's the kind we don't live in anymore. The world that used to give us puzzles but now dishes up mysteries. And no amount of data about yesterday will solve the mystery of tomorrow. Yet, as we've already noted, large organizations are designed for stability and control, and are full of people with veto power over new ideas and initiatives. They are the "designated doubters." The few who are allowed to try something new are expected to show the data to "prove" their answer and get implementation right the first time.

Designers have no such expectations. Uncertainty is mother's milk to them. They thrive on it—hence their enthusiasm for experiments and their patience with failure. Design teaches us to let go and allow more chaos into our lives. Designers lean into uncertainty, while managers often deny or fight it. Not all managers, though. When we studied managers who had succeeded at organic growth, we found a distinctly designer-oriented attitude toward uncertainty.

But it's not raw courage that sets designers apart—it is having a process they have faith in. As one designer told us recently about what he does when he's unsure he can pull off a particular challenge: "I trust the process. It has surprised me many times before." Acceptance is far superior to denial in a world in flux, but success takes courage and more than just a positive attitude. Designers have developed tools—such as journey mapping and prototyping—to help them actively manage the uncertainty they expect to deal with.

Fourth, design understands that products and services are bought by human beings, not target markets segmented into demographic categories. It is easy in business to lose sight of the real people behind the "demand." The reality of human beings and their needs fades as they are tabulated and averaged into categories, reduced to the status of preferences in a conjoint analysis. Lost with that reality is the deep understanding of needs—often ones that aren't even articulated—that is the starting point for profitable growth. This messy reality—that behavior is driven by more than economic logic—is something that designers understand well. They master the skills of observation, of understanding human beings and their needs, while managers learn mostly to evaluate, an activity that rarely involves the kind of empathy that produces fresh insights. Professional doubters are much better at judging than creating. Dr. Alan Duncan at the Mayo Clinic noted: "Until design thinking came to the Mayo Clinic, we were better at poking holes in new concepts than filling them."[7]

For all of these reasons, it's easy to get swept up in the lure of design and the vilification of business as usual, but let's remember why business looks like it looks and acts like it acts. Managers are stewards of other people's resources, so there will always be a need for careful analytical processes that justify strategic investments and for the people whose natural inclinations lie

THE CATALYSTS

Over the past four years a group of colleagues, including Jeanne, have studied managers who have successfully achieved organic growth in mature businesses. They went inside some of America's most prestigious companies to dig into the details of how 50 of these managers achieved their success. They named them the "Catalysts" because, like chemical catalysts, they made things happen—quickly—that wouldn't have happened without them, mostly by virtue of their ability to skillfully navigate in a world of uncertainties and limited resources. They taught us a set of growth lessons.[8]

You don't have to search far and wide to find opportunities. Right under your nose there are opportunities to create better value for existing customers that will enhance your relationships with them. You just have to know your customers very well to see them.

You don't have to bet big in order to be successful. In fact, big bets often cause failure. Place small bets fast, and learn learn learn.

Speed thrills. An obsession with speed drives a surprising and powerful array of positive consequences. Overcoming the lethargy of "business as usual" pays off.

SIX THINGS MANAGERS KNOW ... THAT ARE DEAD WRONG

With or without the benefit of MBA coursework, professional managers tend to follow a set of maxims that simplify their professional lives. Sayings like "Keep your boss in the loop" and "It's sometimes better to beg forgiveness than to ask permission" are good examples. Unfortunately, some of the old, reliable tenets don't work anymore. Here are six common management myths that will definitely make your life more difficult.

Myth 1:
Don't ask a question you don't know the answer to.

This one is borrowed from trial lawyers, and it traveled into mainstream business because it always seems career-enhancing to look smart. Unfortunately, growth opportunities do not yield easily to leading questions and preconceived solutions. A better maxim for growth leaders is:

Start in the unknown.

Myth 2: Think big.

There are always pressures to be sure an opportunity is big enough, but most really big solutions began small and built momentum. How seriously would you have taken eBay (online auctions?) Or PayPal (online escrow?)? In an earlier era, FedEx looked like a niche market. To seize growth opportunities, it is better to start small and find a deep, underlying human need to connect with. A better maxim for growth leaders is:

Focus on meeting genuine human needs.

Myth 3:
If the idea is good, then the money will follow.

Managers often look at unfunded ideas with disdain, confident that if the idea were good it would have attracted money on its own merits. The truth about ideas is that we don't know if they are good; only customers know that. Gmail sounds absurd: free e-mail in exchange for letting a software bot read your personal messages and serve ads tailored to your apparent interests. Who would have put money behind that? The answer, of course, is Google. In that light, a better maxim for growth leaders is:

Provide seed funding to the right people and problems, and the growth will follow.

Myth 4: Measure twice, cut once.

This one works fine in an operations setting, but when it comes to creating an as-yet-unseen future, there isn't much to measure. And spending time trying to measure the unmeasurable offers temporary comfort but does little to reduce risk. A better maxim for growth leaders is:

Place small bets fast.

Myth 5: Be bold and decisive.

In the past, business cultures were dominated by competition metaphors (sports and war being the most popular). During the 1980s and 1990s, mergers and acquisitions lent themselves to conquest language. Organic growth, by contrast, requires a lot of nurturing, intuition, and a tolerance for uncertainty. Placing bold bets falls well short of our proposed maxim:

Explore multiple options.

Myth 6:
Sell your solution.
If you don't believe in it, no one will.

When you are trying to create the future, it is difficult to know when you have it right. We think it is fine to be skeptical of your solution, but be absolutely certain you have focused on a worthy problem. You'll iterate your way to a workable solution in due time. In this case, we propose two design-based maxims:

Choose a worthwhile customer problem.

Let others validate.

in that direction. The organization's "designated doubters" may slow down innovation, but they play an important role in prudent decision making (wouldn't we have loved some more risk-averse doubters in on the Wall Street conversations that got so creative with innovative financial instruments like derivatives?).

An unavoidable but healthy tension exists between creating the new and preserving the best of the present, between innovating new businesses and maintaining healthy existing ones. As a manager, you need to learn how to manage that tension, not adopt a wholly new set of techniques and abandon all of the old. The problem in many established organizations today is not that our analytic approaches are bad—it's that they are all we've got, and so, like the young boy with a hammer, everything looks to us like the head of a nail.

The future will require multiple tools in the managerial tool kit—a design suite especially tailored to starting up and growing businesses in an uncertain world, and an analytic one suited to running established businesses in a more stable one—not two opposing sets wielded by warring groups of people who can't communicate with each other. For some managers, a design approach seems natural. But for most it isn't, in part because managers have literally been taught to do the wrong thing when faced with the uncertainty that surrounds growth.

They've been told to "think big" and not waste their time on the small stuff, to "prove" the value of new ideas using extrapolated historical data, to sit in conference rooms and show

PowerPoints instead of finding a customer in the real world to partner with on a small experiment. Why? Because, again, we've built mind-sets and skill sets attuned to dealing with predictability and control. Not surprisingly, these modes of thinking and behaving get in the way when the environment turns unpredictable and uncertain—the place that growth and innovation inevitably call home. Sadly, managers who rely solely on what they have been taught won't achieve the innovation that their career success depends on.

What managers need is not a right brain transplant that throws the old left brain tool kit away— they need to be taught some new approaches to add to the tool kit they've already got. So before we throw out the baby with the bath water, let's recognize that business as usual can help managers do things designers have trouble with. Design needs business thinking for good reasons:

First, because novelty does not necessarily create value. The flip side of the defense of the status quo because of its familiarity is the pursuit of novelty only because it's new. Profitable growth requires ideas that are not only new but that create value for somebody because of that newness.

Second, because even value creation is not enough. Businesses, to survive, must care about more than just creating value for customers. It is an important, but insufficient, first step. To survive long-term, businesses need to be able to execute and to capture part of that value they create in the form of profits. This requires thinking about issues like how defensible your new idea is against competitors' intrusion and how scalable it is: Can we translate from small experiment to significant business without messing up the recipe? Understanding the value capture piece is often hard for designers but critical to designing profitable new organizational futures.

And third, because how many more stylish toasters and corkscrews do any of us need? Cool stuff is great, but design has the potential to offer so much more. Design has the power to change the world—not just make it pretty. And businesses are some of the most powerful institutions on earth today. We'll build a better planet only if we meld these two ways of working and use them to drive new futures that matter.

So—can business and design build a future together? Let us tell you why we are optimistic that they can. First, organizations similar to yours are doing it right now and making it work, with solid results. And while we've emphasized the differences in our discussion, there are some shared values as well. There is a movement toward convergence around some of the most important questions of all: Why are we here? What is our purpose? Designers have learned

AN ABSURDIST'S TAKE ON THE
LURE OF "MORE NEW COOL STUFF"

As proof that design thinking is ready for a new challenge beyond the making of cool products, we offer Exhibit A: Freddie Yauner's line of extreme (and extremely cheeky) products called Because We Can. *Yauner is a 2007 graduate of London's Royal College of Art, and his product line includes:*

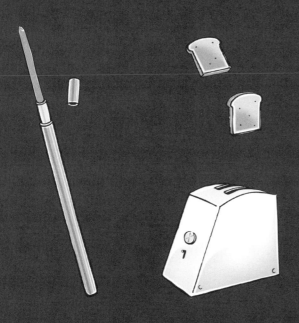

1. A lipstick that lasts an entire year (it is nearly 1 meter long).

2. A clock that tells time so accurately that it is impossible for the human eye to read the last two digits (it comes with an optional camera to capture an image of those two digits so you can know precisely what the time was a few seconds ago.

3. Our personal favorite, the Moaster, a toaster that launches the toast up to 5 meters in the air.

When asked what inspired him to create these objects, Yauner revealed his subtext:

❝ Because we can do a thing doesn't mean we should do a thing."

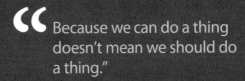

His satirical aim is to poke holes in the notion of "the biggest, the best, the fastest," as a critique of the current state of design and consumerism. The discipline of design, Yauner believes, is ready to address some of the world's most challenging problems, rather than simply produce "objects that pretend to make us better or fulfill our dreams."[9]

that it's not all about cool gadgets and $200 trash cans. Business has been taught the painful lesson that there are some serious downsides to managing the numbers and chasing quarterly earnings per share growth as if it were the holy grail. Increasingly, we are recognizing that the fundamental measure of success—in design and business—is whether we are really creating value for somebody out there. Is somebody's life better (along some dimension of their choosing) because of our efforts? Without that, sustainable profitability is a mirage.

There's also the data thing in common. Sure, we know that managers love it—but there is a pervasive myth that designers don't, that design is synonymous with "winging it." Maybe when practiced by celebrity architects and fashion divas it is, but in the trenches, design is every bit as data-driven as traditional management approaches. It is just a different kind of data: Good designers take the time to make their ideas concrete and go out and get better data from the real world rather than extrapolating data from the past. In doing so, they belie another popular misconception—that a design approach is riskier than a traditional business approach. Quite the opposite is true: Managers need to accept that their basic belief that "analysis equals reduced risk" is just plain wrong in the face of uncertainty. Hiding in your office using questionable numbers from the past to predict the future is just about the riskiest thing you can do.

Uncertainty comes with the territory when your goal is growth. You can't avoid it or deny it and get the growth results you want. But that doesn't mean that you are powerless to do anything about it. You can't make it go away, but you can manage it rather than allow it to manage you.

Let's look closer at how the process and tools of design can help you minimize risk and maximize opportunity in this crazy world of ours.

CHAPTER TWO:

FOUR QUESTIONS, TEN TOOLS

Remember the drawing of the design process in Chapter 1? Here is ours:

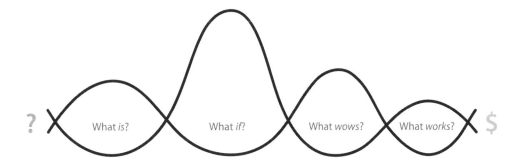

We start and end in the same place as Apple's Tim Brennan, but we've untangled the hairball into a manageable process. Despite a lot of fancy vocabulary like "ideation" and "co-creation," the design process deals with four very basic questions, which correspond to the four stages of the process: **What *is*? What *if*? What *wows*?** and **What *works*?** The **What *is*** stage explores current reality. **What *if*** envisions a new future. **What *wows*** makes some choices. **What *works*** takes us into the marketplace. The widening and narrowing of the bands around each question represent what designers call "divergent" and "convergent" thinking. In the early part of each stage of the design thinking process, we are progressively expanding our field of vision, looking as broadly and expansively around us as possible in order not to be trapped by our usual problem framing and pre-existing set of solutions. After we have generated a new set of concepts, we begin to reverse the process by converging, progressively narrowing down our options to the most promising.

There are ten essential tools that a design thinker uses to address the four questions, to navigate this pattern of divergent and convergent thinking. These are the tools you need to create new possibilities and (equally important) reduce the risk as you manage the inevitable uncertainty of growth and innovation. The rest of this book will unpack each of these stages and tools, and help you apply them to your own growth challenges. First, we want to look at how the process unfolds across the four questions, and how each tool fits within it, acknowledging that this model imposes an artificial linearity on a very fluid process.

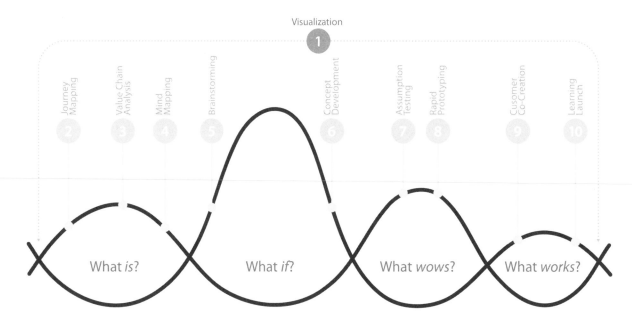

As we get started, we want to call your attention to a very special design tool: **visualization (tool 1)**. This is really a "meta" tool, so fundamental to the way designers work that it shows up in virtually every stage in the process of designing for growth. Often, visualization is integral to the other tools we will talk about. It is an approach for identifying, organizing, and communicating in ways that access "right brain" thinking while decreasing our dependency on "left brain" media such as numbers. Visualization consciously inserts visual imagery into our work processes and focuses on bringing an idea to life, simplifying team collaboration and (eventually) creating stories that go to the heart of how designers cultivate empathy in every phase of their work and use it to generate excitement for new ideas.

What *is*?

Step Away from That Crystal Ball

All successful innovation begins with an accurate assessment of the present, of current reality. We save the crystal ball for later. Sounds counterintuitive, doesn't it? When we think of something new, we usually think of the future—not the present. Why not start there?

For a lot of reasons: First, we need to pay close attention to what is going on today to identify the real problem or opportunity that we want to tackle. A lot of managers throw away all kinds of opportunities for growth before they even get started by framing the problem too narrowly. For years, product developers at P&G focused on improving the detergents that were used to clean floors. One day they realized (with the help of design thinking) that what their customers really wanted was cleaner floors, and that could be achieved through means other than better detergents—such as a better mop. That insight produced a runaway bestseller in the form of the Swiffer, a growth initiative that revolved around a product invented in the middle ages (if not before). Fruitful searches go back to the basics: What is the job to be done?

A funny thing often happens as we pay closer attention to what customers are up to—we find that the clues to the new future lie in dissatisfactions with the present. And not just when the innovation you are looking for is incremental. Ultimately, growth is always about solving customers' problems—even

THE TEN TOOLS

1. **Visualization:** using imagery to envision possibilities and bring them to life

2. **Journey Mapping:** assessing the existing experience through the customer's eyes

3. **Value Chain Analysis:** assessing the current value chain that supports the customer's journey

4. **Mind Mapping:** generating insights from exploration activities and using those to create design criteria

5. **Brainstorming:** generating new possibilities and new alternative business models

6. **Concept Development:** assembling innovative elements into a coherent alternative solution that can be explored and evaluated

7. **Assumption Testing:** isolating and testing the key assumptions that will drive the success or failure of a concept

8. **Rapid Prototyping:** expressing a new concept in a tangible form for exploration, testing, and refinement

9. **Customer Co-Creation:** enrolling customers to participate in creating the solution that best meets their needs

10. **Learning Launch:** creating an affordable experiment that lets customers experience the new solution over an extended period of time, to test key assumptions with market data

if they don't yet know that they have one. But if you pay close enough attention to their lives and their frustrations, you might see what they don't. You've got to meet your customers where they are today in order to take them where you think they need to be. So the most promising place to start any growth search is to find out what customers don't like about today—and identify the trade-offs they'd rather not have to be making.

This is precisely the approach that executives at Pfizer Consumer Healthcare used to address one of their growth challenges. Nicorette, the company's leading smoking cessation product, had reached a plateau. Pfizer was unhappy with Nicorette's performance, in every sense of the word. Its sales and profits had stagnated. Perhaps even more disturbing—it just didn't seem to be working very well. Pfizer executives estimated that smokers made seven unsuccessful attempts before they finally kicked the habit. Not good enough, in their view. So Pfizer set a goal of growing the brand significantly—in both sales and performance. In contrast to a "business as usual" approach, the Pfizer team chose to use design thinking to find growth.

The Nicorette team started by selecting a group of customers to get to know better. Pfizer executives chose to focus on a group of customers who were likely to be open to change: young smokers. Their biggest growth market for this target group was in Europe, so they set up a team based in London. In taking a design thinking approach, the Pfizer executives committed themselves to developing a deep understanding of the underlying behaviors of these smokers—beyond the

CHRISTI ZUBER

Christi Zuber describes herself as "a nurse with a passion for design." After practicing nursing in outpatient surgery and home health, she got a master's in Health Administration and joined Kaiser Permanente, one of the largest health care providers in the United States.

Christi was first exposed to design when one of Kaiser Permanente's executives saw the infamous IDEO shopping cart video. He asked Christi if IDEO's design thinking methodology could be replicated in-house at Kaiser Permanente. Maybe so, she thought. So, she recruited a handful of pioneers (none with a design background) and took on her first project, looking at prenatal services and the journey of an expectant mother.

DESIGN THINKER

> "A lot of us are taught critical thinking—and the belief that if we go into a conference room with enough intelligent people we can come out with the perfect answer. Doing this made me realize that there is never a perfect answer, and you won't come up with one that is close by sitting in a conference room. You've got to get out and get hands-on with what you are trying to do. You've got to be involved with the people you are trying to change the experience for, to understand what their real needs are."

simple fact that they were chemically addicted to nicotine. They observed their daily lives, following them home and to their offices, trying to understand how both their cigarette habit and their attempts to quit fit into the bigger picture of their lives, the meaning these held for them. This research uncovered a surprising insight: The smokers who wanted to quit did not think of their habit as a medical problem. They didn't want to take pills to "cure" it. Instead, they viewed smoking as a lifestyle choice they had made and wanted to gain more control over. They believed that, one day, they would make a different choice, quitting eventually. Once Pfizer managers understood how their customers framed the smoking cessation issue, they felt confident that they would be able to design more effective offerings for them.

In Section II of this book, we look in-depth at exploring the present. First, we focus on the customers we hope to serve. Design offers a number of ethnographic tools, such as customer **journey mapping (tool 2),** to help us assess an idea's potential for value creation. This tool teaches us how to "follow customers home" and develop a deep understanding of their lives and the problems they struggle with, so that we can bring our organizational capabilities to bear on the ones in our sweet spot.

It is also important in our explorations to assess the potential for value capture (that is, profitability). So we need to do a deep dive on the value chain in which this new idea is likely to be implemented. Who are the powerful players? What are their incentives? Will they want and be able to help us? Accurate information on your organization's own capabilities and resources (and that of key competitors) is also essential. And we'll want to recognize early on the capabilities we are missing and locate the right partner to provide them. All this involves a **value chain analysis (tool 3)**.

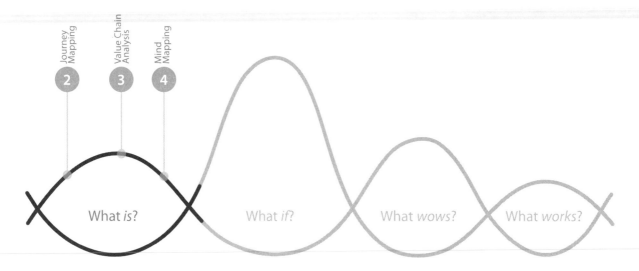

In our Pfizer example, the research produced important insights, not just into how smokers framed their "problem" but also around the larger issue of what it took to kick the habit. The Pfizer team realized that Nicorette usually did not work as well in isolation; success involved a multipronged program involving counseling, hypnosis, or some kind of clinic or support group. None of these seemed like opportunities that would leverage the organization's strengths. Pfizer would need to position itself in a new value chain, alongside partners that could provide complementary offerings.

When do you know that you've explored enough? This is always a judgment call. There is a deluge of low-quality information available from sources like the Internet. But high-quality information usually requires field research, which is expensive and time consuming, so we don't want to chase data we don't need. Figuring out what you need is not always easy. But keep in mind that the primary objective in this exploration stage is not to build a "business case" for any particular idea. That comes later. The purpose here is to prepare to generate ideas—not evaluate them.

Designers have come up with a number of tools for looking for patterns in and making sense of the wealth of data we've amassed in this exploratory stage. One approach is what we call **mind mapping (tool 4)**, which helps organize the mass of information we've collected and draw insights from it about the qualities of the innovations we need. We then use these design criteria to generate ideas in the next stage.

What *if*?

Pursue Possibilities

Having synthesized the data and identified emerging patterns, ideas begin to pop into our heads of their own volition. We start to consider new possibilities, trends, and uncertainties. Even without consciously trying, we are beginning to develop hypotheses about what a desirable future might look like. And so it is time to move from the data-based exploratory **What *is*** stage to the more creativity-focused question, **What *if*?** We'll do this in Section III.

At this stage, we are staring the future in the face. And we are tempted to ask, "Where did I put that crystal ball?" We begin to wonder (borrowing the words of historians Richard Neustadt and Ernest May) where the future might divert from the familiar flows of the past, how our insights could translate to new possibilities.[10] Designers call this stage *ideation*.

To generate truly creative ideas, it is crucial to start with possibilities. Often in business, in our attempts to be "practical," we start with constraints. This is deadly to breakthrough thinking. If we start by accepting all the things that don't allow us to do something better, our designs for tomorrow will inevitably look a lot like those for today. Our only hope for real creativity is to ignore some key constraints in order to identify a new set of possibilities. Then the real creativity kicks in—figuring out how to get those constraints out of our way. It takes a lot of momentum to do this—and that gets created in a good possibilities discussion that energizes the hard work of overcoming constraints. In many of the business innovations we have been involved with, the creativity that really matters lives in *how* the new future was accomplished, not *what* it looked like. As poet Eric Hoffer observed, there are few incentives to creativity more powerful than being told that you cannot have your own way.

During the **What *is*** stage, we looked at how customers currently frame their problems and the mental models and constraints that we impose on them. Now we'll use this information to formulate hypotheses about new possibilities.

Pfizer executives hypothesized about a new approach to reaching out to customers: What if, instead of presenting doctors in lab coats helping smokers with a medical problem caused by a chemical addiction, the company could offer coaches in sweat suits encouraging smokers to adopt a different training regimen? Pfizer knew that it also needed to incorporate Nicorette into a multifaceted smoking cessation program that would address not just the addiction but broader lifestyle choices. The company hoped to find a way to achieve this without investing in bricks-and-mortar elements, like health clubs and clinics. Eventually, the team found a small firm in Scandinavia that had developed a behavior modification program based on tailored reminder messages, delivered via cell phones.

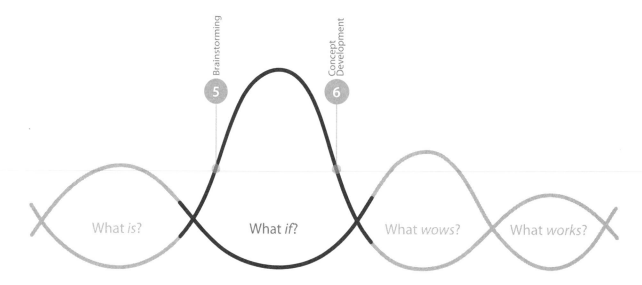

We will approach the ideation challenge using a familiar tool, **brainstorming (tool 5)**, although we will apply it with more structure than the free-form approach often used. A disciplined approach to brainstorming is crucial to overcome its inherent pitfalls. A key reason that brainstorming is unfulfilling is the lack of a formal process to convert the output into something valuable. Another design thinking tool we introduce here, **concept development (tool 6)**, will take the output of the brainstorming process, organize it into coherent clusters, and architect the most compelling clusters into a robust "concept." We moved from data to insights in our first phase; in this one, we'll move from insights to ideas to concepts. Ideas often fit onto a Post-it note, but a concept requires a poster.

DIANE TY

Diane Ty spent ten years at American Express, in product marketing and new product development. With an undergraduate degree in political science and an MBA from the Wharton School, she had no formal exposure to design until she went to work for AARP and took on the challenge of helping twenty-somethings think about retirement — using design thinking tools to get there.

Diane didn't want to fall into the trap of brainstorming many ideas that would never be pursued. For her, the value of the design thinking tools is in the clear steps to pursue, improve, and validate concepts with users.

"My background is very consumer focused. I have experienced the classic ideation several times, the kind where you bring together a bunch of colleagues and you brainstorm lots of different ideas. I was always disappointed when you got to the point of trying to see if any of the ideas were actually feasible, able to be implemented. Design thinking was an approach that was interesting to me because it was different from typical ideation."

DESIGN THINKER

Now, having developed some hypotheses (in the form of concepts) about new possibilities for creating value for our customers that might lead to profitable growth, we'll begin to think systematically about prioritizing the concepts we have come up with and figuring out what wows.

What *wows?*

Find the Sweet Spot

If all has gone well in the preceding stages, we probably have far too many new concepts to move forward all at once. A firm we worked with recently generated more than 300 ideas of interest, which they narrowed down to 23 concepts. Of these, only five were eventually moved forward into marketplace testing during the **What *works*** stage. Clearly, much prioritizing must be done. We need to make some choices. And so in Section IV we move from our **What *if*** hypothesis-generating mode to a **What *wows*** strategy for culling our concepts down to a manageable number. We are looking for those that pack a potential "wow," that hit the sweet spot where the chance of a significant upside in customer value meets attractive profit potential. This is the "wow" zone.

This necessitates starting with some kind of evaluation of the only data we've got—data about today. Again, keep in mind that we are not "proving" the value of an idea; we are just ready to do some thought experiments to begin to assess what the business case might look like. Because it is often difficult to assess the long-term potential of a new concept, we want to tread carefully so that we don't unintentionally favor the incremental concepts and dismiss the more radical ones.

The good news is that we have an approach at our disposal that has been little used in business but is far more useful in assessing early-stage innovations than the much maligned but still commonly used metrics like return on investment (ROI) and payback. This is the good old scientific method. The scientific method uses both creative and analytic thinking. That is what makes it such a useful tool when we want to be imaginative in the search for possibilities and rigorous in figuring out which ones to pursue. Unlike brainstorming, it doesn't ask us to leave our analytic minds at the door. It invites both the left and the right brain into the process, and it is custom-made to deal with situations involving a lot of unknowns. It accomplishes all of the above by treating our new concept as a hypothesis and then testing it.

It starts with the hypotheses generated by the **What *if*** question we've just talked about. Then it takes these new possibilities (which are really educated guesses about something we think is likely to be a good idea) and tests them by asking "Under what conditions would that hypothesis in fact be a good business?" Or—worded differently—"What would need to be true for my concept to be a good one?" The idea is to surface and test the assumptions underlying each hypothesis. The hypotheses that "pass" this first set of tests are good candidates for turning into real experiments to be conducted in the marketplace. And so **assumption testing (tool 7)** is one of the most potent arrows in the designer's—and the manager's—quiver. Remember, the goal here is not uncovering "truth"—it is making better choices under conditions of uncertainty.

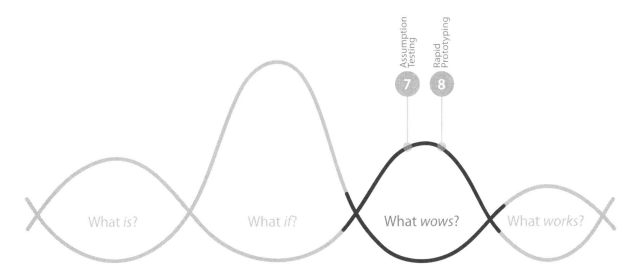

All design is essentially hypothesis driven, which, in the design world, is shorthand for saying that the solutions generated are the outcome of an iterative rather than a linear process. That is, design starts with a tentative solution and expects to improve it through experimentation. Think of an architect's progress through a series of representations of his or her work—sketches, to cardboard models, to wooden models, to perhaps 3D models these days—all before a single shovelful of dirt has been lifted at the construction site.

So having tested our assumptions as carefully as we can, given existing data, it is time to move to the real thing—experimentation in the marketplace, which allows us to collect real-time data on our new concept. In order to do this, we need to take the concepts that have successfully passed through our screening process and translate them into something actionable—a prototype. **Rapid prototyping (tool 8)** a new business idea seems like a challenging task. Even the words sound formidable. But all we are talking about here is taking the concepts generated in the **What** *if* stage that have passed our screening tests and turning them into something concrete enough to spur conversations with important stakeholders (like customers and partners). Our intent here is to create visual (and sometimes experiential) manifestations of concepts. By giving our concepts detail, form, and nuance, we can better facilitate meaningful conversation and feedback about what needs improvement.

Prototyping should be robust and fast. Designers talk about "low-fidelity" prototypes, which are just good enough to share with those whose opinions we value. This is all we need, because we prototype to *learn* rather than to *test* a theoretically finished product. This allows us to make mistakes faster, identifying areas that can be improved while agreeing on what's working effectively. A strong prototyping phase can identify and correct potential problems and will ensure a smoother implementation. As Frank Lloyd Wright noted, it's easier to use an eraser on the drafting table than a wrecking ball on the building site. Regardless of the form that prototypes take, the focus is on capturing details of how the model will work and how people will experience it. Remember the goal: creating a compelling story that makes sense and makes the idea feel real to your collaborators.

At Pfizer, the team created a prototype of a new behavior modification program by combining the Scandinavian firm's IT platform, tailored to smoking cessation, with other elements of the business model, such as increased user interactivity and social networking elements like family support. Each of these elements was prototyped using tools like screen shots and story panels. Customers were asked to walk through the interfaces and provide their reactions to the design team.

What *works*?

Time to Get Real

Finally! We are ready to launch and learn from the real world. First we'll try out a low-fidelity prototype on some customers and see how it goes. If it succeeds, we'll build a higher-fidelity prototype of our idea and see if any customers are willing to part with their money for it. This is our focus in Section V.

A particularly powerful approach to determining what works involves inviting the customer into the conversation in an active, hands-on way. The tool we'll use here is **customer co-creation (tool 9)**. There is no more effective way to reduce the risks of any growth initiative than to engage customers in designing it.

Improved prototype in hand, we are now ready to move into the marketplace. To accomplish this, we will offer a tool we call a **learning launch (tool 10)**, which moves your developing concepts into the field. As you design the launch, you will want again to be explicit about the search for disconfirming data. This is the information that disproves your hypotheses. It is the most valuable information to find—and the easiest to miss. To enhance your ability to detect it, you must lay out in advance what disconfirming data would look like.

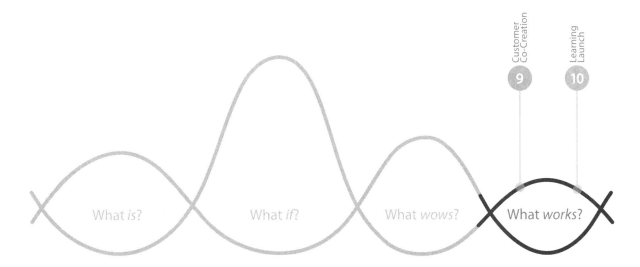

Included in the learning launch is attention to another important task: designing the on-ramp. How do you launch your new offering in a way that will best persuade customers to give it a try? Without trial, all that value creation potential is only that—potential. So you will need to pay attention to how you get to awareness of your new offering, and from there to trial.

As you proceed, keep in mind some of the principles of this learning-in-action stage: Work in fast feedback cycles. Minimize the cost of conducting your experiments. Fail early to succeed sooner.

Test for key trade-offs and assumptions early. Most important, play with the prototypes in the field instead of defending them.

The Pfizer team tested three different on-ramp approaches: putting the offering on a retailer's shelf, selling it through intermediaries like employers or insurance providers, and selling direct over the Internet. To the executives' surprise, the offering sat on retail shelves and went nowhere. Selling through intermediaries proved to be too slow to meet growth targets. The third option, the Internet, emerged from the learning launch as the big winner, though Pfizer had never used this channel before.

Before we walk you through the ten tools in greater detail, there is one more ingredient you will need to become a successful design thinker.

The Project Management Aids

To succeed at harnessing the power of design thinking to grow your business, you need to do more than try out the ten tools of design thinking: You have to *manage* the growth project itself. This is not as easy as it may sound. You are gathering large amounts of data, dealing with significant ambiguity and uncertainty, and working with new internal and external partners—all under the pressure of deadlines and resource constraints. With all these new tools and new types of data, this train can easily come off the tracks.

To make sure that it doesn't, we will introduce four project management aids (PMAs) in this chapter as well. (Turn to the Appendix for more-detailed descriptions and templates.) The PMAs are not design tools—they are not about generating or testing ideas. Instead, they are communication protocols that link the design thinking process to the established project management structures of the organization. They will help you control the project by systematically capturing the learning from each stage, codifying decisions and transitioning from one stage to the next, and integrating the results into a successful growth project. The diagram to the right shows the purpose of each project management aid and how they fit together.

DESIGN BRIEF

Project Description
Intent / Scope
Exploration Questions
Target Users
Research Plan
Expected Outcomes
Success Metrics
Project Planning

DESIGN CRITERIA

Design Goal
User Perceptions
Physical Attributes
Functional Attributes
Constraints

NAPKIN PITCH
CONCEPT NAME

| NEED | APPROACH |
| BENEFIT | COMPETITION |

NAPKIN PITCH
CONCEPT NAME

| NEED | APPROACH |
| BENEFIT | COMPETITION |

NAPKIN PITCH
CONCEPT NAME

| NEED | APPROACH |
| BENEFIT | COMPETITION |

LEARNING GUIDE

Strategic Intent
Remaining Key Assumptions to Be Tested
In-Market Test Plan — Untested Assumptions / Success Metrics
Financial Capital to Be Expended

LEARNING GUIDE

Strategic Intent
Remaining Key Assumptions to Be Tested
In-Market Test Plan — Untested Assumptions / Success Metrics
Financial Capital to Be Expended

PROJECT MANAGEMENT AID	PURPOSE
PMA 1 **Design Brief**	• Formalizes the growth project • Defines goals, resources, timelines, etc. • Serves as a "North Star" throughout the project
PMA 2 **Design Criteria**	• Sets criteria to evaluate alternative designs (derived from study of user needs and business requirements) • Becomes part of the design brief
PMA 3 **Napkin Pitch**	• Crystalizes communication of solution concepts (after brainstorming and concept development) • Describes each of the best few (3–5) solutions that meet the design criteria in a template that allows for apples-to-apples comparison
PMA 4 **Learning Guide**	• Defines an affordable level of resources to invest in learning whether (or not) the top 2–3 concepts are feasible

The bottom row of our design thinking model (below) shows where each PMA fits in the process.

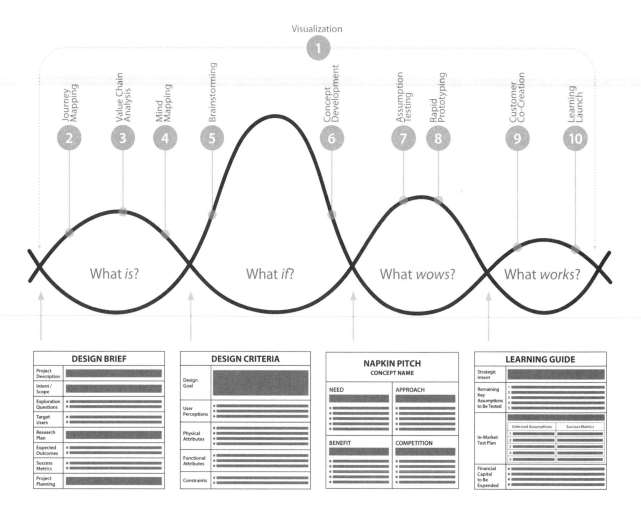

And that's the design thinking process: four questions, ten tools, and the project management aids. That's all there is to it.

Warning!

Incorporating design thinking into your search for growth is going to take some patience on your part. Most companies, however well intentioned and excited about innovation, aren't P&G and Google; they still don't "get it." Chances are that yours is one of those. All kinds of obstacles will probably be thrown your way while you are being asked to find profitable new growth opportunities. That challenge—moving a design project through an organization—is the subject of our final chapter.

Managers trying to innovate and grow new businesses in big bureaucracies need all the help that they can get. And design really can help. Big time. So let's get started on showing you how.

SECTION II:
What *is*?

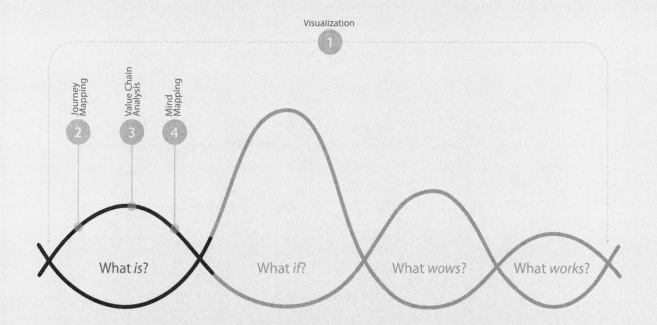

Visualization
1

Journey Mapping
2

Value Chain Analysis
3

Mind Mapping
4

What *is*?

What *if*?

What *wows*?

What *works*?

As managing director of strategic marketing development at AARP, a nonprofit organization dedicated to serving Americans over the age of 50, Diane Ty faced a common challenge: how to cultivate future members among the next generation while serving current ones. The catch here was that the AARP name was virtually synonymous with "retirement," a distant concept for many Americans under 50.

Founded in 1947 by a former high school principal who wanted to help retired teachers find health insurance, AARP had grown into an organization of more than 40 million members. Despite dramatic social changes in the second half of the twentieth century, it remained focused on its founding principles: promoting independence, dignity, purpose, and quality of life for older persons. Like any organization with an eye on the future, it was concerned with positioning itself for a new generation of members likely to be quite different from the current one.

Enter Diane Ty, a Wharton MBA with a background in both consumer products and the nonprofit world. Her assignment, dubbed Project Prepare, was to explore this question: What could AARP provide of value and relevance to young people, given the close association of the brand with the over-50 set?

Diane and her team started with the hypothesis that young people—Gen Xers and Gen Yers—would want to receive services over the Internet, but they had no preconceived notions about what services to focus on. Having never served this demographic group, they had little research on it. And so they started their exploration with secondary research. What they learned was sobering:

> "We took a snapshot of what today's gloom and doom looks like through the eyes of young people: They are graduating from college with on average more than $4,000 in credit card debt and over $20,000 in student loan debt, and they are coming into a workplace where there's been flat wage growth. A large number of them are unemployed or underemployed. Many don't have health insurance. Defined benefit plans are being replaced by defined contribution plans, and only half of today's workers are eligible to participate in these. Even if they are, many do not take advantage of the employer match, and many don't have the financial acumen to even know how to invest on their own. And then look ahead and see the questions around Social Security … This is a perfect storm."

Diane's team learned on further investigation that this economic insecurity among the young was having a profound impact on AARP's current members:

> *"What we found was astounding. Seventy percent of our members today are still supporting their adult children in some way financially. And we know that our members have not saved enough for retirement. So they're struggling with their own plans around retirement, they're struggling with caring for their elderly parents, and then they find themselves still supporting their adult children."*

Diane wondered what AARP could do to get young people on a path toward economic security. "We were open to anything," she said. "Do they want a membership group? Do they want help getting health insurance? Anything."

In order to move forward amid all the uncertainty, Diane decided that she and her team needed a much deeper understanding of those in Gen X and Y, "their hopes, dreams, aspirations, challenges, issues, and concerns."

They started by selecting 30 people between the ages of 18 and 49, asking them to keep a written journal and take photos. The team also took photos and video footage of their home environments and conducted in-depth interviews about their dreams, challenges, and fears. What emerged from this exploration were three distinct segments among the under 50s: 18-to-24-year-olds, whom the team called "finding your bliss"; 25-to-34-year-olds, called "reality hurts"; and 35-to-49-year-olds, whom they termed "maintenance mode."

Believing that it would be difficult to create a single value proposition compelling to all three segments, the team decided to home in on the "reality hurts" group as an initial target. Diane explained why:

> *"This group was really interesting to me. They're emerging from that total dependence on their parents and the artificial environment of school, and they're coming into the real world. And how do they respond? The decade of 25 to 34 was when most significant life events were occurring. And each life event tended to be a catalyst for a money decision: starting your career, getting married, buying a house, having a child, changing a job, dealing with divorce. It was a huge group of events."*

Within this age group, there were again distinct segments, such as the "achievers," who were already doing the right things financially and were ready for services like retirement planning, and the "overwhelmed," who were too focused on getting out of debt to begin thinking about the future.

Diane and her team began looking across the data they had amassed about the needs of people under 50 and considering how AARP could meet them. The team wanted to capitalize on AARP's capabilities and assets, including its extensive network of financial advisors, who might be willing to donate their services because of AARP's reputation and nonprofit status.

AARP had other strategic objectives, as well. First, the organization wanted to be seen as an unbiased, trusted advisor to this demographic—this meant, Diane's team learned, avoiding the appearance of "selling" anything. In addition, the organization did not want to replicate or compete with services that already existed in the marketplace. Finally, AARP wanted to focus on those who needed help the most, rather than serving those who were already in good financial shape.

We believe that this initial phase of AARP's Project Prepare conveys what a well-constructed **What *is*** stage looks like. The team began with a **design brief** (project management aid 1) that clarified the scope of the project, its intent, the questions it hoped to explore, and the target market it wanted to explore them with. We talk more about the components of a good design brief in the Appendix, but—for now—check out page 46 to see what Project Prepare's starter design brief might have looked like.

Team members also remained focused on AARP's business objectives and the strategic opportunities and vulnerabilities the project was meant to address. In fact, you might argue that their lack of prior knowledge about the under-50 set was a plus—it encouraged them to jump into the study with questions instead of answers.

They then gathered a lot of data from various sources, including the people they wanted to serve. They took an ethnographic approach to their target customers, digging deeply into their lives. And they were willing to live with the uncertainty and the challenge of making sense of all they learned, translating it into insights that allowed them to identify design criteria for the next stage: idea generation. Their patience in the face of not knowing brings to mind one of our favorite quotes, which comes from Tim Brown, CEO of IDEO:

"The biggest barrier is needing to know the answer before you get started. This often manifests itself as a desire to have proof that your idea is worthwhile before you actually start the project … The assumption that you've got to have a business case … before beginning to explore something kills a lot of innovation."[1]

Of course, AARP's in-depth study of the 30 Gen Xers is just the beginning of the Project Prepare team's customer research. This deep qualitative research into a small number of potential customers' lives sets the foundation for the broader, larger scale research that will come later.

Since the goal of design is to envision and implement an improved future state, it is always tempting to jump right to it—to the future, that is. Indeed, many people believe design thinking starts with brainstorming; some even think it ends there! But as Diane Ty's story illustrates, the design process starts squarely with the here and now. Innovative ideas are generated from insights about current reality. Without those insights, the imagination starves. What ideas would a band of AARPers, uninformed by the kind of research Diane Ty and her team conducted, have come up with if they had started with brainstorming? We can't know for sure, but we suspect the kind of ideas that have given brainstorming a bad name in management circles.

There is a lot packed into the **What *is*** phase. This is where the framing takes place and, in fact, where most design thinking projects are won or lost. Think of the frame as the foundation of a house. Every elegant flourish on the upper floors depends on it. When you stop to ask, "What is?" you may find that you can look at the problem through an entirely new lens. What you thought customers truly wanted turns out to be less attractive. And so you must reframe your project.

By taking the time to develop deep insight into the problem or opportunity and its context, design thinking establishes the reference point for change, the constraints that shape it, and the criteria for what success looks like.

Tools in This Section

What *is* starts with the creation of the design brief and ends with the identification of design criteria. Between those two project management aids are four design thinking tools: **visualization**, **journey mapping**, **value chain analysis**, and **mind mapping**.

DESIGN BRIEF
We can imagine that AARP's Project Prepare design brief would have looked something like this:*

Project Description	AARP may be able to improve relevance to its core market (Americans 50+) by helping adult children (Gen Y and Gen X) achieve financial independence and "PREPARE" for their futures.
Intent/Scope	The initial scope will focus on better understanding the needs of Gen Y and Gen X. AARP will then explore both for-profit and nonprofit approaches to meet their needs—with the project's primary goal being positive social impact. AARP will pursue a for-profit approach if and only if AARP can use its resources to create a new market space that will serve the public good. Opportunities for AARP may include: health insurance challenges, college debt burden, retirement planning, building credit, and/or improving credit card habits.
Exploration Questions	The project will inform key strategic questions including: 1. What is the demographic/psychographic with the greatest need? What do these needs look like? 2. Can AARP provide services to Gen Y and Gen X in a way that reinforces its mission to make life better for Americans over 50? 3. Should AARP provide services to the public or only to the adult children of AARP members?
Target Users	At project kick-off the target audience includes all Gen Y and Gen X. We intend to align on a more focused target based on ethnographic research and strategic discussion.
Research Plan	We will screen Gen Y and Gen X research participants, in order to select the 30 most relevant subjects to follow up with an in-home interview.
Expected Outcomes	We expect to discover several high-potential opportunities for AARP PREPARE to: 1. Ensure Gen X and Gen Y have the resources to age and retire with dignity 2. Build AARP's relevance to 50- to 65-year-old Americans by serving their children 3. Build AARP's relevance to younger Americans to ensure future membership levels.
Success Metrics	1. Did we discover a compelling reason to PURSUE or NOT PURSUE this target market at this time? 2. Did we find any high-potential needs or demographic/psychographic segments that represent a compelling opportunity for AARP? 3. Have we identified the design criteria that a service must meet to address these opportunities?
Project Planning	A 3-person full-time team will conduct the "exploration" phase over a 10-week time frame.

*All statements, numbers, and timelines within this document are the supposition of the authors and do not reflect the actual design brief used within AARP.

As you read about each tool, think about the dynamic relationship among them. When they come together successfully, they will point the way toward opportunities that were always there but were hidden. They feed the imagination for the next stage: **What** *if*.

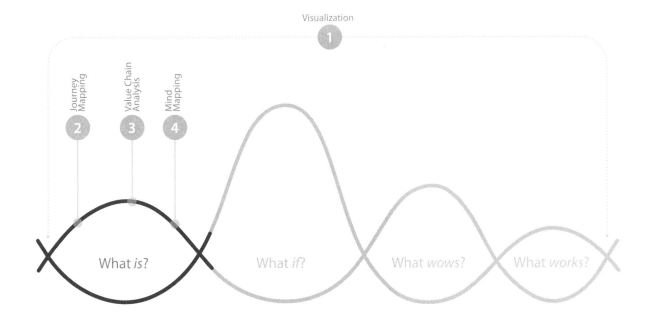

SWISSCOM'S CHRISTINA TAYLOR ON THE IMPORTANCE OF REFRAMING

Christina Taylor, who heads the brand experience area at Swisscom, Switzerland's leading telecommunications services provider, talked about the importance of considering the framing of a project:

"A group of our engineers argued for the need for a router in every Swiss home to power wireless access. Such a router would have the latest technology and the intelligence to locate and choose the network that has the best access and coverage. It was a purely tech-centric project. In my department, it is our job to look at what people really need. So we went to visit customers' households. Most importantly, we took the managers, the decision makers, along.

We saw that the biggest problem the customer had with the new router is that this thing looked ugly, and he doesn't want it. He doesn't want cables especially hanging out of it. It has to look good and solve the cable problem. If your telephone plug is in your living room and it has this ugly gray thing hanging there with three black cables sticking out of it, it's not Swiss. Our houses are proper and neat and then to have this ugly thing in a well-designed living room? And so we reframed the project itself: It's not the router that people want, we argued, but access to the digital world. We are not selling a box; we are providing access to the digital world.

We then built a very different prototype, which included a new box, solving the cable problem, and designing the experience along the whole customer journey: how you ordered the box, how you installed it, and all that.

I think the end result would have been very different without reframing. It would have been just another router, a wireless box hanging on the wall."

CHAPTER THREE:
VISUALIZATION

Visualization is the transformation of information into images that you see, either literally with your eyes or figuratively with your mind's eye. Sometimes it's about representing text or numbers or other bits of data with pictures (which, as you may have heard, are worth a thousand words). Sometimes it's about assembling scattered ideas into a compelling story that can generate vivid mental images. In either case, conjuring up visual depictions of customers and their experiences makes them human and real. Visualization makes ideas tangible and concrete, often sweeping away ambiguity with the stroke of a pencil. It brings a different part of your brain into play; it's a different way of knowing. Visual approaches needn't be complicated or sophisticated. Simply drawing pictures on a whiteboard can be a powerful exercise.

When to use it: Visualization is the "mother of all design tools." You will use it in every stage of the design thinking process. During **What *is*,** you'll use it to document and make sense of your observations of customers and their journeys. In **What *if*,** it will help you capture new concepts. In **What *wows*,** you'll use it to make your concepts tangible. And in **What *works*,** it will let customers help you test and refine them.

Why visualization de-risks your growth project: Making your work visible reduces project risk substantially— and is especially important for effective cross-disciplinary collaboration—because text is much more open to varying interpretation than pictures and stories (which use words to paint a narrative picture). When you explain an idea using text, the rest of us will form our own mental pictures, usually informed by our training. And, of course, that's what kills us: We each go off and do our own thing, on the basis of what your words meant to us. Later you may say, "That's not what I was talking about!" If instead you present your idea to us by drawing a picture of it or telling a story, you reduce the possibility of unmatched mental models. This is no guarantee that we will all agree with your idea, but now at least we will know what we are disagreeing about. Visualization also reduces project risk by build-

DESIGNER ANGELA MEYER ON VISUALIZATION

"Visualization is really important throughout the process of design. For example, we might rely heavily on photography when we're doing our exploration activities. So we're researching, we're trying to understand our users, we're looking at customers, we're looking at new user segments. Photography is a very rich way for us to understand that world, and not just the people themselves but the context in which they live.

When we move on to looking for patterns, that's where we start to think visually, to take what we've learned in our exploration phase and begin to synthesize it. And synthesis itself is a visualization process.

When you get to concept development, visualization becomes incredibly key, because concepts are literally coming out of your imagination and your brain is creating pictures of something that doesn't yet exist. It's creating pictures of something that will soon be, and the way that we use visualization in that is often through sketching. We might use a whiteboard and work as a group and use sketching and diagramming to capture our thinking. We might use photographs at that point to make sure that we understand what the customer experience is like.

As we move forward into prototyping, we get much more detailed in the way that we start to visualize. We create very complex diagrams, our maps of how we think the customer experience ideally is going to work. Pictures and images enable us to not only help people understand what it is we're trying to do but to help convince them of the worthiness of that particular idea or the strength of that concept.

The advice I would give to businesspeople interested in improving their visualization skills would be just to practice. It can be a little intimidating at first. But I think that people will find that once they start getting in the habit of doing that, you quickly see how the rest of the room responds to you when you get up and start drawing."

ing commitment to the solutions we will create together. The more vividly we are able to visualize the future we want, the more likely we are to soldier on through the slings and arrows our execution efforts inevitably face.

We've all heard about the differences between the "left brain" and the "right brain." The left brain, we're told, is analytic and logical. It likes numbers and language. The right brain contributes much of what makes us human, such as emotion and intuition. It also is an expert at synthesizing ideas and seeing connections between them. Current brain science tells us it's not quite that simple, but right brain/left brain is still a useful metaphor for understanding the different ways we make decisions. According to that metaphor, visualization—the vivid depiction of ideas—is a right brain tool. And although neither the right nor the left brain is superior to the other, we often exclude the right brain from our business deliberations.

We know intuitively that seeing something helps make it real. Recent brain science studies have taken us a step further in understanding *why* visualizing ideas and activities is so important—they have demonstrated the existence of *mirror neurons*. Only humans and orangutans are known to have these neurons (hence, monkey see, monkey do), which rehearse the physical steps of an activity or expression we observe without sending a command to our muscles to execute those steps. In one experiment, for instance, scientists found that research subjects used the same part of their brain when they watched a film clip of a disgusted individual and when they themselves

MODERN BRAIN SCIENCE

In the 1830s, it was commonly believed that man descended from angels. By the 1860s, most educated people believed that man was a hairless ape (thanks, Darwin!). The field of economics has been undergoing a similar tectonic shift during the past 30 years, as our understanding of how people make choices has moved from economic utility toward so-called "behavioral economics." Modern brain science has added fuel to the fire. In the mid-1990s, a new diagnostic tool—the functional MRI (fMRI)—became widely available and has been driving a new understanding of how the brain works during decision making. Here are some of the most striking findings from modern brain science:

Left and right is *wrong*. The fMRI shows that the left brain is not responsible for analytics, and the right brain is not responsible for creativity. Actually, the brain is more like an archeological dig. The outermost layer, the neocortex, is the youngest. It is the seat of logic, math, and speech processing. The next layer, the limbic brain, is the seat of emotion. All mammals have this, which is why we bond to dogs and dogs bond to us. The oldest part of the human brain is the brain stem or "reptile brain." It mediates survival functions such as heart rate and breathing.

The brain is an argument. We make different decisions in different ways. In addition, different parts of the brain respond to stimuli in different time frames. Think of two teams of lawyers doing discovery to prepare for a trial, and you've got the picture. The fMRI scans support the notion put forward by Jonah Lehrer that the brain is an argument.[2] How we settle that argument depends on social context, prior experience, etc.

We have a low say-do ratio. Our responses to questions often fail to match our behavior. For example, if I asked you whether you would accept free e-mail in exchange for letting an algorithm read your private messages and serve you tailored ads, you would probably say no. And yet Google's Gmail does exactly that.

We respond quickly to feedback. When a team of researchers sent reports to homeowners comparing their energy consumption to that of other homes in their neighborhood, the high consumers immediately reduced their consumption, even though no behavior change was requested. Low consumers, on average, maintained their frugality. The feedback alone drove down consumption.[3]

Thoughts trigger feelings—and actions. Harvard psychologist Ellen Langer conducted a study in which she asked people to come to a test center and take a reading comprehension test. Group A read about disabled or injured people. Group B read about extreme athletic achievers. The first group walked back to their cars more slowly than they had when they arrived. The second group walked more briskly. The mere contemplation of infirmity led Group A to emulate infirm behavior![4]

All of the above point to the conclusion that we humans are *adaptive opportunists*. Why is this good news for design thinkers? First, design thinkers don't seek answers through analytics, so we are not susceptible to our inherent weaknesses as rational calculators. Second, they rely on direct observation of *behavior* (ethnography), which yields insights that are more valid. Third, design thinking relies heavily on visualization, and modern brain science tells us that visualizing is a natural precursor to *doing*. And finally, design thinking relies on trial-and-error, which is perhaps the most essential tool of adaptive opportunism.

were exposed to a noxious smell.[5] Observing, it turns out, does more than activate our visual perceptions; observed actions are mapped onto our motor systems. So if you are watching someone hitting a baseball, you're actually practicing your swing in your head. You are working all the neurological connections that you need to actually stand up and swing the bat. And so *seeing* can be a powerful enabler of *doing* (as well as a powerful enabler of empathy).

Getting Started

One of the great things about most design thinking tools (including visualization) is that they require very modest capital investment: a whiteboard and markers, flip charts, and Post-it notes, in this case. More-advanced aids like PowerPoint software, digital cameras, and camcorders can be handy as well. Designers use sophisticated software such as Illustrator and Photoshop, but mastering these isn't necessary for reaping the extraordinary benefits of visual thinking. A trained designer who knows them, however, is an absolutely invaluable addition to the team. Here are some basics to get you started, using an example from Christi Zuber at Kaiser Permanente:

1. **Keep it simple.** Make your visual representations as simple as possible. Stick figures can often do the trick. Use color in a meaningful way. Keep clip art simple and avoid the clutter of multiple fonts and other fancy effects. Remember—this is not about displaying your artistic ability; it's about starting to turn your ideas into reality. Creating visuals that are too polished can backfire when your goal is to solicit feedback.

    Christi Zuber's team used a simple visualization exercise in a project at Kaiser aimed at reducing medication errors:

    "When we'd ask nurses how medication administration was, they'd say it was fine. Knowing it wasn't, we asked them to sit down and draw medication administration. As clinicians, we are trained to use our left brain to an extreme degree. So we gave them markers and paper and asked them to sit down and draw pictures. It was amazing—totally different than hearing them say, 'It's just fine.' In their drawings, they were in this big hurry. They would write out words like interruptions: it would be a nurse on roller skates with his or her arms full and all these other little stick figures asking them questions. So we took all that and started looking at the themes coming out of this."

Designers use drawing to help them "think out loud." Once they see an idea on paper, they can add to it, build on it, keep it in their notebooks, and share it with others. Designers make a fine art of this type of quick sketching, but it requires little more than stick figures, arrows, hearts, stars, boxes, and the occasional wheel.

2. **Break your problem down into components.** In his bestseller on visual thinking for managers, Dan Roam argues for visualizing the following components: who, what, how much, where, when, how, and why.[6] Ask members of your team to work individually to create visuals of each component and then share them to create a group version.

> The Kaiser nurses drew themselves in the middle of administering medication, capturing the who, what, where, and how of the activity.

3. **Think in metaphors and analogies.** Metaphorical thinking is the process of recognizing a connection between two seemingly unrelated things. A metaphor is a trick of language perfectly designed to share an open thought process with others and to identify and communicate a deeper set of relationships and possibilities.

> The nurses' metaphorical drawings of stick figures on roller skates conveyed that, despite their declarations, all was not fine. They felt that they were moving precariously fast and could lose control.

4. **Use photographs.** Photographs can be enormously helpful for capturing information, making it real, and communicating it to others. Think of a bullet on a PowerPoint slide from a financial services organization that says, "Our clients have an average of more than five different accounts." Now think of a photograph of a man's wallet stuffed with credit cards and another of his desk littered with bank statements. What is the difference in impact between the line of text and the photographs? Can you marry words and pictures for maximum communication impact?

> Christi described how she and her team combine multiple visualization tools, including stories and photographs, to make sure people are sharing their observations with one another:
>
> *"After we do observations, we won't let too much time go by before we actually take those observations and put them in stories. Each story is one PowerPoint slide. Not a long complicated story, but a fairly simple story that will have a representative image, maybe of the space that we were looking at or of the person we were talking to, and then maybe a very brief paragraph of two or*

three sentences of what that story was. This causes you to sit down and capture things outside
of your own personal notes. Transparency is a really important thing. If you let things float in
your own head for too long, you start to fall in love with them and create your own reality."

5. **Experiment with storyboarding.** Storyboards are nothing more than a series of panels that sketch out a sequence of events. They are a fundamental tool for visual thinking. Storyboarding involves just six simple elements:

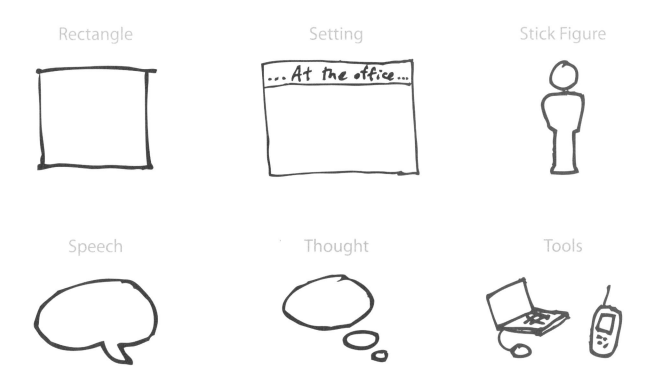

The rectangle provides your frame, and its background creates your setting. Stick figures represent your characters, and speech and thought bubbles capture their words and thoughts. Finally, you may want to include the tools that they use. We'll return to storyboarding for this chapter's "Try This at Home" assignment.

6. **Create personas.** Personas are fictional characters, created out of the insights from your exploratory research, that can exemplify certain attributes. Because they make the potentially abstract concept of "customer" very personal and human, personas enhance your ability to build the empathetic understanding of customers that is at the heart of design thinking. In Chapter 4, we'll talk more about developing and using personas. For now, just think of creating some characters and bringing them to life with photographs and descriptions.

Meet Eric G

- Eric is a 73-year-old with glaucoma.

- Eric doesn't use his glaucoma prescription, which means his eyesight will slowly deteriorate into blindness.

- Eric does not feel afraid when his optometrist tells him that any eyesight loss he experiences cannot be recovered, because Eric knows the decline is gradual.

- He thinks if his eyesight starts getting really bad he will get another prescription and deal with it then, when it's absolutely necessary.

- Eric dislikes touching his eyes for any reason. That's why he's never used contacts, despite requests from his wife. He also hates using the prescription eye drops.

- Eric says he has decided that saving money is more important than filling a prescription for a nonurgent condition. He admits that he is worried about whether he and his wife have enough money to last for their retirement.

ANDRE MARTIN OF MARS INC. ON STORYTELLING

"Storytelling has always been a part of business. It's just that now we're overtly talking about it as a *tool* that leaders can use.

Storytelling is the difference between solving a problem and creating a cause. Lists solve a problem: Here's an issue we face, let's create a pro and con list about how to solve it and then pick the best option. A cause is something that ignites people and unites people. That is what a good story does: It creates a cause.

I think business leaders are bored with 90 percent of the conversations they have in a day. They sit there and have PowerPoint after PowerPoint, and meeting after meeting, and to-do list after to-do list. And they're looking to be inspired. Business leaders want a little bit of data, a hard fact, and some recommendations. The space between that and how you get to those things is where storytelling can be compelling.

There's a variety of stories a leader can tell in an organization. When we talk about design thinking, the story is about driving transformation. In this story, the main character is the big wicked problem facing the organization. And so first you have to *sell the challenge*. You have to help the audience understand how the current state is more dangerous than any other possibility out there. You have to get them in the frame of mind that they want to take this on and make this challenge a cause they can invest in. Then you have to be able to talk very intelligently about the *fellowship*, the people involved in the challenge, whether they are customers or other stakeholders. Then you have to give them a chance to talk about the *tensions* that exist. If you can present those tensions, you create a place where people want to get involved because they want to have that debate and that conversation. Finally, you have to present the *possibilities*—there is a way to get this solved.

Storytelling allows you to get people to pay attention for just a little bit longer, with a little bit more diligence and energy. I think that's important. If you can raise the level of engagement in your business, you will do wonders for your performance."

7. **Tell stories.** Storytelling is just what you think it is: weaving bits of information into a narrative (one that may be a bit longer than you'd find on a storyboard) rather than just making a series of points. Like many visualization techniques, storytelling is something that managers already do. All good presentations—whether analytic or design-oriented—tell a persuasive story.

    Storytelling accelerates your ability to sell design thinking by helping you make your ideas feel real to sponsors, customers, partners, and funders. It reduces the chances of one of the heartbreaks in innovation: never being allowed to try. Like visual images, stories allow you to access emotion and emphasize experiences. They make ideas concrete, tangible, and personal. They add the richness of context and allow you to "sell" a problem as well as its solution to those who must give it the green light. They build identification and empathy with their characters and help managers develop a personal investment in their welfare. With any luck, they keep their audience awake.

    You tell me that we should be giving aid to Africa, and I'm not too excited. But if you tell me that you've adopted a six-year-old boy named such-and-such in this village and you're now giving him clean water, I can picture that child.

    There are different kinds of stories, and each is told differently. There is usually a customer experience story as well as a business story. But we should never separate the stories from the data—they need each other—just as we should never exclude analytic thinking, or design thinking, from our tool kit.

8. **Practice guided imagery.** Guided imagery is the creation of a particular kind of story, one that takes a listener on an inner journey, helping the listener to visualize more vividly what you're saying. This technique has been used for decades in sports, leadership training, medicine, and other fields to inspire peak performance. Visualizing new possibilities, or current realities, as vividly as possible contributes to our ability to execute change successfully. Beginning with the end in mind, visualizing the possibilities as clearly as we can, as Stephen Covey famously advises, can be a powerful aid in the innovation process. Whether you're conjuring up a redesigned customer experience or the travails of a customer navigating your current services, engaging the imagination and emotion of your audience can make a big difference in your success as a leader of innovation and growth.

Remember Dave Jarrett, our accountant from Chapter 1? He is a big fan of guided imagery, tracing it back to his experience as a facilitator of a workshop based on Stephen Covey's *Seven Habits of Highly Effective People:*

> *"The visualization process that we use with clients is based on some of the training we did in the Seven Habits. People actually can visualize these concepts if they just take themselves out of their normal setting. Covey helped me to really understand how powerful visualization is. A group of accountants and systems guys will tell you they can't do that. They'll tell you they are very concrete thinkers; give me facts, give me figures, and I'll give you an answer. But they are perfectly capable of thinking in that mode if they just let go of the fact that they are used to seeing a computer screen or a set of books and records. That's part of what has made me an advocate for design: going through that process and understanding how powerfully people can create these things in their minds and how vivid and real they become to them."*

Visualization techniques may seem foreign to those of us who've spent years exercising our left brains. But take heart—you already know the basics of how to do this. Charts, graphs, and PowerPoints are visualizations, after all. You just need to graduate to a broader and more inventive set of images. And remember that the basic information you communicate may not change, but the way you communicate it will.

Try This at Home

We'd like you now to go back and use the six simple storyboarding elements we talked about to tell the story of how you proposed to your significant other (or how you were proposed to, or how you met). Plan to use four frames for the storyboard:

- Frame 1: Before, part 1
- Frame 2: Before, part 2
- Frame 3: During
- Frame 4: Immediately after

Here is an example (an appropriately humble one) that will help you get started.

Don't make it a masterpiece! Limit your drawing time to 15 minutes and then share it (in all its imperfect glory) with your significant other. Or even ask him or her to draw a version and compare the two.

What did you notice about the process of creating this storyboard? It's hard to restrict the story to four frames, isn't it? Figuring out the core parts of the story is always challenging, but your audience will thank you.

What did you notice about your significant other's reaction? Did it make a connection with him? Did it cause her to reflect on the event, perhaps even revise it a bit? If the two of you each drew a storyboard, how are they similar and different? What can you learn from this?

Want more practice? Play Pictionary with your friends, family, or coworkers on a regular basis. A weekly competition will increase your visual thinking capabilities exponentially.

CHAPTER FOUR:
JOURNEY MAPPING

Journey mapping is the representation, in a flowchart or other graphic format, of the customer's experience as he or she interacts with your company in receiving its product or service. These maps can depict the customer's actual or ideal journey. Either way, plotting its stages forces you to focus on your customers, rather than on your organization. As you map their journey, you're walking a mile in their shoes. Along the way, you are looking for the emotional highs and lows and the meaning that the experience holds for the customer. These are the key to identifying value-creating innovations.

During **What** *is*, journey mapping leads you through your customer's current experience, facilitated by data gathered through observation and interviewing. In doing so, it seeks to shift how you understand that experience. It provides a compelling description of unmet needs and helps you group the differences among customers and, in the process, identify opportunities for improvement. It is never about "proving" that your ideas are worthwhile (journey mapping is a no-selling zone). Instead, this tool is aimed at exploration that will yield ideas for future prototyping.

When to use it: Create the journey map as one of the first activities during **What** *is*, to document the existing customer experience and isolate the highs and lows. In the **What** *if* stage of a growth project, the journey map can help you generate ideas during brainstorming. During concept development (also part of **What** *if*), maps of ideal rather than actual experiences can be created to identify the novel elements of the concept and determine how to create them. Finally, during **What** *wows*, the journey map provides the elements for prototyping the new experience.

Why journey mapping de-risks your growth project: If we could add only one design tool to a manager's repertoire, it would be journey mapping. The number one reason growth ideas fail is that we misjudge what customers want. The surest way to de-risk a project is to develop a deeper feel for that. Journey mapping gets you closer to customers' lives, to their problems and frustrations, as you seek to understand how to create value for them. This knowledge is the most important input to the search for profitable growth.

As recently as a decade ago, we would invite groups of customers into an air-conditioned room with a one-way mirror, where they would succumb to groupthink and inexact memory. Today, designers have adopted the methods of anthropologists, observing customers in their natural settings and using techniques like journey maps to capture what they see and hear. Focus groups conducted with the users of Tide laundry soap, for example, reported high satisfaction with the packaging. When researchers went into their laundry rooms, however, they found quite a few washing machines with soap-encrusted screwdrivers nearby. "I use that to get the box open," the subjects said.

The journey map is a powerful tool to shift your focus from "What does my company want?" to "What is the customer trying to do?" It invites problem-solving teams to form a strong empathetic connection with the customer, not as a data point or a demographic, but as an individual with hopes and challenges worth considering. This field is sometimes called *social research* or *design research,* and it rewards patience, thoughtfulness, and reflection. An experienced social researcher encouraged us to "listen gently" and resist the temptation to declare a quick victory.

Emotions are a central focus here, offering powerful clues to what is really going on inside our heads (and hearts). Dr. Jill Taylor, a former Harvard Medical School brain researcher, noted:

> *"Sensory information streams in through our sensory systems and is immediately processed through our limbic system. By the time a message reaches our cerebral cortex for higher thinking, we have already placed a 'feeling' upon how we view that stimulation—is this pain or is this pleasure? Although many of us may think of ourselves as* thinking creatures that feel, *biologically we are* feeling creatures that think.*"*[7]

Operations experts advise managers to "staple yourself to an order" to understand the flow of activities within your firm.[8] We're suggesting that you instead "staple yourself to a customer." It may change what you believe about his or her order.

Getting Started

Here's how journey mapping typically works, illustrated with a recent journey mapping project undertaken at the Darden School of Business:

1. **Select the customers whose experience you want to understand more fully.** Spend some time investigating the context in which they do the "job" that your offering contributes to. Secondary data sources like websites and blogs are often a good place to begin.

   A faculty/student team undertook the mapping of the MBA student's journey at Darden. The aim was to improve the educational experience and increase student satisfaction. As team members began the project, they reviewed a wealth of published information about this generation of students.

2. **Lay out your hypothetical view of what the customer's journey looks like from beginning to end.** Be sure to include all steps in the journey, not just the ones in which your firm participates.

   The MBA mapping team identified 12 key steps in the MBA journey, beginning with the decision to investigate getting the degree and ending with graduation.

TIPS FOR INTERVIEWING

1. Put the interviewee at ease. Let him or her ask you questions.

2. Ask for stories and examples. Capture memorable quotes.

3. Be curious. Look for surprises and inconsistencies and probe these.

4. Use silence. Don't be afraid of it.

5. Pay attention. Gesture and tone can say more than words.

6. Paraphrase. Don't lead the witness.

7. Listen hard for inefficiencies, overexertion, and workarounds.

WATCH THIS! BEHAVIORS TO LOOK FOR DURING ETHNOGRAPHY

Ethnography involves observing users in their natural context. That sounds clear enough. But what are we looking for? As you watch users interacting with your products or services, here are some behaviors to look for:

Confusion: Watch the users' facial expressions. A confused look signals an opportunity to make the experience more intuitive.

Overexertion: Notice moments when people must work too hard (even if they don't realize it) as they seek to solve their problem.

Pain Points: Look for moments that are acutely unpleasant or annoying. You will see it in users' facial expressions and body language.

Appropriation: Appropriation is the use of a product for a new purpose. Plastic milk cartons are often appropriated by college students to serve any number of functions.

Skipped Steps: If users skip a step, it might signal that they don't need, want, or understand the value of that step.

If you don't understand what you saw, you can always ask. Just save the asking for later, because your observation is often more valid than users' explanations; they are often unaware of their behaviors.

3. **Identify a small number of customers (generally 12 to 20)** representing the range of demographic attributes of interest to you.

> 16 Darden students, representing a cross-section of age, gender, nationality, marital status, and educational background, were identified.

4. **Conduct a few pilot interviews.** Using your hypothesized steps, ask the customer to walk you systematically through the journey to be sure that you are accurately capturing the steps and getting the kind of data you need. This is hard work—harder than you think. It is often necessary to probe a single step repeatedly in order to get your interviewee to reflect more deeply on what they were thinking and feeling and why. Don't settle for superficial answers. Keep pushing (gently).

5. **Finalize the questionnaire** on the basis of what you learned from the initial interviews and conduct the remaining interviews, focusing on the emotional highs and lows of the experience. We find it best for two researchers to interview one subject together. This allows the interviewer to give the interviewee his or her full attention while the second researcher takes notes.

6. **Identify the essential moments of truth and other themes from the interviews.** This is an intense phase of sense making. You begin by asking interviewers to summarize what they learned during each interview on a single template. Then you rip a sheet of flip chart paper down the middle and write the name of each interviewee across the top. As a team, you summarize the key emotional highs and lows as bullets on the flip chart. You then post these on a wall so that you can begin to look for themes.

The Darden mapping team prepared summaries of all interviews and began searching for patterns and insights.

7. **Study the themes you have uncovered** to identify a number of dimensions, usually psychographic rather than demographic, that you believe help reveal the differences in your data. We find a list of universal human needs, compiled by the Center for Nonviolent Communication, to be very useful in generating dimensions and have included it in the Appendix.

The Darden mapping team identified the following potentially differentiating dimensions:

introvert ←→ extrovert

footloose ←→ outside obligations

embrace debate ←→ avoid debate

culturally malleable ←→ culturally rigid

ask for help ←→ help yourself

high confidence ←→ high humility

laser focus ←→ open exploring

extension of college ←→ extension of career

▶ identify with dominant culture ←→ identity with micro culture

▶ pragmatist (career advancement) ←→ purist (holistic learner)

A more-sophisticated version of journey mapping continues by creating a set of personas:

8. **Select the two dimensions that you feel are most revealing.** This will create a 2x2 matrix, in which each quadrant represents an archetypal persona.

The Darden team created the matrix using the two dimensions selected:

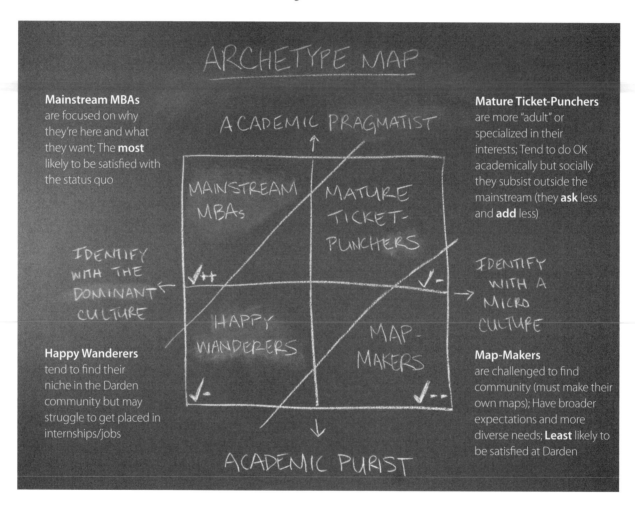

Mainstream MBAs are focused on why they're here and what they want; The **most** likely to be satisfied with the status quo

Mature Ticket-Punchers are more "adult" or specialized in their interests; Tend to do OK academically but socially they subsist outside the mainstream (they **ask** less and **add** less)

Happy Wanderers tend to find their niche in the Darden community but may struggle to get placed in internships/jobs

Map-Makers are challenged to find community (must make their own maps); Have broader expectations and more diverse needs; **Least** likely to be satisfied at Darden

9. **Position each interviewee into one of the quadrants.** Describe the archetype as fully as possible, focusing on the demographics and psychographics that make this archetype unique.

Here is one of the personas the MBA team invented, using the bottom left quadrant:

Scott, the Happy Wanderer

- Scott enjoys Darden and assumes that getting a job will be easy with a degree from a top-tier school—as long as he does well in his courses.

- Scott has a BS from Cornell in mechanical engineering.

- After two years at a rewarding engineering job, Scott was told by the head of his department that he'd need a graduate degree to advance in the company.

- Scott applied to top-tier business schools and was accepted by several. He chose the one with the best weather and facilities.

- Scott focuses on his course work and enjoying club activities with peers more than on job-search activities.

- Scott is an extrovert, which occasionally helps him do well at recruiting events, but he doesn't have a strategic approach to the events; he mostly goes for fun.

Managers often want to know what percentage of the market a given persona represents. That is not the purpose of personas: They are not meant to represent actual target market segments. They are *devices,* meant instead to reveal deeper insights into the various kinds of experiences that customers are having and to help generate innovative ideas about how to improve those experiences.

10. **Map the journey of each persona.** Each persona should reveal its own set of low points. These are the "pain points" that represent the most valuable innovation opportunities for that customer type. Some low points may be shared across personas, making them a particularly fruitful target for innovation.

Here is Scott, the happy wanderer's, Darden journey:

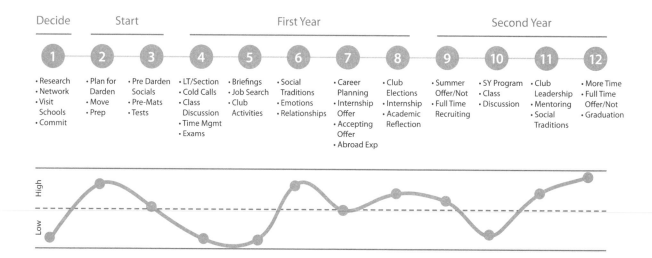

Looking at Scott's journey map, we can make many observations. For example, his three most significant pain points involved his decision about what school to attend (too many choices), the job search (again, too many choices and not enough time to pursue all of them *and* study), and some classroom issues (other students are not as committed to their studies). All suggest fruitful innovation opportunities.

The MBA journey mapping project gave faculty an insight into the lives of students that profoundly altered many of their beliefs about the Darden experience. After a presentation by student members of the mapping team, one long-tenured faculty member commented, "I've learned more about the real lives of our students in the last hour than I have in the last 20 years!"

Faculty began, in particular, to appreciate that the experience was holistic yet very different for different students. For all students, what happened in the classroom, on the job market, or at a happy hour party were part of the same overall experience. This drew attention to the significance of the work of non-academic colleagues in areas like Student Career Services. Having previously dismissed the job search as a necessary evil, faculty began to see it was perhaps *the* most significant factor in students' experience at Darden—and that the disconnect between classroom activities and those related to the job hunt was a prime source of dissatisfaction. They also saw that different students needed and expected radically different things from that search process. Scott, for instance, needed a lot of upfront counseling to help him set some priorities. The "mature ticket-punchers," on the other hand, entered Darden focused on a particular career and needed a very different kind of attention. This new understanding of students' current experience—as seen through their eyes—laid the foundation for significant innovation and ushered in a new level of collaboration between faculty and Career Services staff.

Journey mapping differs substantially from market research tools such as focus groups and surveys. Managers trained in those methods are often uncomfortable with the findings of ethnographic data because the number of subjects is much smaller. But a small sample is a deliberate choice, because the data gathering is deep and intense. The process uses observation and intensive interviews (ideally done in real time, while the customer is in the middle of the experience), in which the researcher walks the customer through each element of an experience, using open-ended questions. These may be supplemented by photo diaries and videos.

Like visualization, journey mapping does not produce generalizable or statistically significant results; it does not "prove" anything. Instead, it spurs creative thinking about the unarticulated needs of customers, often inaccessible using methods with larger sample sizes. Its aim is not to produce a set of recommendations for action; rather, it is to produce a set of *hypotheses* for testing.

Try This at Home

Pick an everyday process, such as taking your child to school in the morning. Follow these steps to map the journey. Remember, the focus is on representing **What** *is*, not on brainstorming new possibilities.

1. List eight to ten steps in the process, starting with "Child wakes up" and ending with "School day starts."

2. Take an 8 1/2-by-11-inch sheet of paper and orient it horizontally in front of you. Draw a horizontal line across it, towards the top of the page. Plot the eight to ten steps as points on the journey represented by numbered circles. Above each step, label the person or institution that is primarily responsible.

The resulting map contains the full sequence of steps but shows the entire journey as neutral. Now we can make some judgments about the experience.

3. Start by drawing a large rectangle below the journey map that runs the length of the journey. Divide the rectangle in half horizontally. On the left side of the paper, label the area above the horizon line as emotional high points and the area below as low points. This will let you capture the range of emotional highs and lows.

Now you will map the emotional highs and lows of the journey from your child's point of view.

4. Draw the best case scenario of the emotions that your child would experience throughout the journey. If everything went smoothly, what would be the best parts? Which parts would still be negative emotionally? Make a list of three or four emotional high points you have observed (or heard about from your child) and plot those points along the journey in the "emotional highs." Label each high point with a short description, such as "gets to sit next to friend." Connect the dots of the best case scenario with a smooth blue line.

5. Next, draw the worst case scenario of the emotions that your child would experience throughout the journey. If everything went wrong, what would be the worst parts of the journey? Which parts would still be positive emotionally? Start by making a list of three or four emotional low points and plot those points along the

journey in the "emotional lows" box. Label each low point with a short description, such as "misses the bus." (Note: A key step can often contain emotional highs and lows.) Connect the dots of the worst case scenario with a smooth black line.

6. Reflect on your work. Now the journey map reflects multiple dimensions: Sequence, responsible party, and emotional variability. Look at the entire map and see what jumps out at you. Which steps have low points but not high points? What might be some unmet needs for your child? For you? Where do *your* emotional low points occur?

7. As the final step in the process, make a list of two or three possible unmet needs for you and for your child. As a reference, consider these ten needs from Center for Nonviolent Communication's list of universal human needs:

Connection	Physical Well-being	Peace	Autonomy
Affection	Rest/sleep	Ease	Choice
Consideration		Harmony	Independence
Inclusion		Inspiration	
Safety			

The goal isn't to nail it; the goal is to identify new hypotheses that may help you reinvent the process. For what it's worth, an acquaintance told us her daughter came up with the idea of wearing her clothes to bed in order to have enough time in the morning to wake up gently and eat a proper breakfast before school. An unorthodox solution, but one that met the needs of that family!

CHAPTER FIVE:
VALUE CHAIN ANALYSIS

Value chain analysis is the study of an organization's interaction with partners to produce, market, distribute, and support its offerings. From it emerge important clues about your partners' capabilities and intentions and your firm's vulnerabilities and opportunities. It is the business-side equivalent of customer journey mapping—it highlights the "pain points" and opportunities in the organization's experience working with upstream and downstream partners to deliver its product or service. Value chain analysis can be useful at multiple levels. You can focus on the value chain in which an opportunity currently resides. You can also explore the value chain of the broader industry.

When to use it: Conducting an end-to-end value chain analysis is an important part of the exploration phase in the search for profitable growth opportunities. You don't want to begin the **What *if*** stage not knowing what makes a new business model attractive to your firm and which parts of the existing model are worth protecting. Value chain analysis also helps you view the market from the perspective of partner firms, potential partners, and competitors (just as journey mapping helps you see through the eyes of the customer).

Why value chain analysis de-risks your growth project: As we said in Chapter 1, creating value for customers is only part of the equation for business success. To be sustainable and attractive, new businesses must create value for the organization (usually in the form of profits) as well as for partner firms. That means new offerings have to be hard for competitors to copy and possible for you to scale. They also need to be something you can execute with your current capability set (or with the help of interested partners). Ideally, they leverage your organization's distinct capabilities. An analysis of today's value chain can give you important insights that will allow you to assess, during the **What *wows*** stage, the likelihood that your new ideas will meet those criteria. A deep understanding of how current suppliers work together to create value, and who has the power to demand a significant share of the profits, is key to helping you avoid committing to a new offering that may create value for customers but is not likely to be profitable for your firm.

Value chain analysis looks more like the kind of classic business analysis you may be used to. It takes you from the customer-centered foundation you established during journey mapping to the business side—the market ecosystem in which the customer's journey occurs. Such an analysis often reveals an industry's "dominant logic": the set of unarticulated rules and beliefs that guide the behavior of firms as they work to fulfill customers' needs. Challenging this dominant logic (a topic we'll discuss in more depth in Chapter 7) by altering the firm's footprint in a way that brings better value to customers or higher bargaining power to the firm can be a prime source of growth opportunities. Combined with journey mapping, it will ensure a broad view of the innovation landscape and lay the foundation for your growth concept's customer and business case.

Value chain analysis becomes an invaluable reference point in the next stage, **What *if***, as we reject the status quo and look for new, innovative ways to meet the customer's need in a more compelling way. Use this tool to spot the inefficiencies that are ripe for rearrangement—typically by shifting the boundaries of who does what in the value chain.

Because value chain analysis is a tool you are probably already familiar with, we will cover it quickly here. We include it to underscore how important such a strategic business perspective is to a successful growth initiative.

Getting Started

Value chain analysis begins by specifying the outcomes the chain creates for the end user and then works backward to include the capabilities and bargaining power of all key participants. We will work through the steps of the analysis here, using PC industry dynamics as an example:

1. **Draw the value chain for your business.** This involves laying out each cluster of activities, working backward from the end point of the value proposition delivered to customers. These clusters, taken together, form the basic architecture of the chain. Each competitor will have its own "footprint" in the chain, its own configuration of activities. Some firms may participate in only one cluster; others will span multiple clusters.

   An important, and often tricky, task is defining what constitutes an element in the chain. Remember that we are mapping strategic clusters of activities, not companies. For a first pass, it is always better to make a more detailed map. You can later collapse clusters of activities that do not need to be viewed separately. If you start out very broadly, you may miss important activities that are invisible at too aggregated a level but could be broken apart to create strategic advantage.

A typical value chain might include these kinds of clusters:

Remember also that we are introducing an artificial linearity to the process, as these activities do not occur in a single stream or in the same order each time. Designers (and some businesspeople) prefer the term "ecosystem" for just this reason.

To appreciate the significance of understanding your value chain as you make growth decisions, consider events of the last decade or so in the personal computing value chain. PCs moved into mainstream use in both business and the home in the early 1990s. At the time, the major component suppliers for a PC were microprocessor, software, and other peripherals manufacturers. These components were assembled by "box" manufacturers and sold to end users through mega computer retailers such as CompUSA. Sales representatives from each of the large manufacturers handled corporate sales. All these players worked together to deliver the final value proposition to end customers: the functionality of personal computing. Two distinct ecosystems, or value chains, emerged. One consisted of IBM and so-called IBM clones. The other was Apple. The IBM computers used Microsoft and Intel products. Apple went its own way. Even though many believed the Microsoft system to be inferior to Apple's in terms of user friendliness and functionality, the ability of other manufacturers to reverse-engineer IBM-compatible computers drove down the price and drove up the popularity of the offerings in the so-called "Wintel" ("Windows" and "Intel") chain. Market share estimates were hard to come by, but estimates are that by 1985, IBM-compatible machines had grabbed half the market share. By 1994, they had topped 90 percent.

2. **Analyze the competitive environment** in each box, identifying the key players and their relative market share.

    For over two decades, component suppliers such as Intel (microprocessors and chip sets) and Microsoft (operating systems and applications software) have dominated the Wintel chain, while the box assembly manufacturers such as Hewlett-Packard, IBM, and Compaq have traded market share and struggled to differentiate their offerings against both one another and a generation of clones that arrived on the scene in the mid-1990s.

3. **Identify the core strategic capabilities** needed to produce the value in each box. What does each contribute to creating value?

    As we assess the key strategic capabilities in the chain, the source of the box manufacturers' profitability problems becomes apparent. The core technical capabilities driving Intel and Microsoft's success are hard to replicate, given their scale, skill, and barriers to entry. The box manufacturers, on the other hand, are involved in what is mainly an assembly operation on the production side. Their differentiating capabilities, it seems, would have to rely on sales and service, but no player in this cluster seems to have a clear competitive advantage.

4. **Evaluate the bargaining power and influence of each player.** Who drives performance? How easy would it be to find a substitute for each player's contribution? How much value does the end user perceive that each player contributes?

    It is easy to see IBM and Hewlett-Packard as competitors. But their partners are also potential competitors. They compete to divvy up the profits generated by the chain, and each is vulnerable to others' growth moves, which can benefit some players and hurt others. Their ability to garner a large share of the profits is a function of their bargaining power and influence in the chain. In the personal computer, the real intelligence rests in the processor because it is the part responsible for executing commands. Its speed determines how quickly a command is executed and hence how fast a computer can work. The user-friendliness of the software and operating system determine how much a user likes the computer. Therein lies the power of Intel and Microsoft.

5. **Determine the possibilities** for improving your power and profitability in the chain. Having analyzed the chain as it exists today, consider what you've learned about the relationship between power and position in it. What determines how value is captured? Who has power? Why? Where do you see opportunities for improving your power and profitability by altering your footprint? These questions set the stage for generating the design criteria used to evaluate growth possibilities.

> By 1993, Dell had become one of the top five computer makers in the world, succeeding where IBM and Compaq had failed by offering a new and unique value proposition—customized configuration and direct sales—and by parlaying its strength in the weakest part of the chain, distribution. Dell's business model, and the footprint in the value chain through which the company executed it, was quite different from that of the less successful box competitors. Dell carried virtually no inventory of parts, dealt directly with customers, and received payment in advance, resulting in a very advantageous cash flow. This allowed the company to post return on investment numbers equal to those of Intel and Microsoft.

6. **Assess your vulnerabilities.** It is important to play defense as well as offense here. Where are you vulnerable to others who might change their footprint in ways that put you at a disadvantage?

> We need look no further than the devastation Intel wrought on its partners with the seemingly innocent Intel Inside campaign to bring home the importance of a clear understanding of strategic vulnerability as an important input into the process of designing for growth. Under the guise of co-branding, Intel's ad campaign effectively demolished barriers to entry and made it very difficult for even the well-known players in the box business at the time—IBM, Compaq, and HP—to differentiate their products. After all, if what mattered was Intel inside, why pay more for Compaq's outside? Eventually, IBM exited the business and Compaq was acquired by HP—not because of competitive moves on the part of other box manufacturers but because its own suppliers commoditized the box. Apple survived the lean years (before the Mac renaissance) by remaining differentiated and retaining control of its value chain, reaping higher margins even on lower volumes.

7. **Identify themes** related to bargaining power, capabilities, partners, and defensibility.

As this cautionary tale emphasizes, analyzing the existing value chain often offers important clues about the most attractive positions, how to capture your fair share of the value the entire chain creates, and how to avoid the forces of commoditization. You need to consider all these elements when deciding where to place your growth bets.

Making the business case

What is the potential value capture of different roles in the network?

• Who drives performance?
• Who has customer loyalty?
• Where does the strategic intent align and diverge?

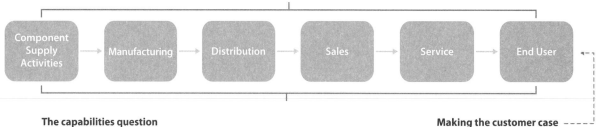

The capabilities question

For each activity cluster in the value chain, what skills and processes are needed to succeed?

Making the customer case

How does the network create and enhance value as *defined by the customer*?

The positioning question

Where are we vulnerable?
What possibilities exist to shift/strengthen our role in ways that improve our ability to create and capture value?
What new capabilities do we need to develop or improve to do this?
Who should our partners be?

When you put together the hypothetical qualities of an attractive opportunity on the business side, and add insights from other sources like journey mapping, you've got a formula for specifying the key attributes of both the customer and the business case for your innovation. We'll move on to that process with the next tool: mind mapping.

CHAPTER SIX:
MIND MAPPING

Mind mapping is the term we'll use for the process of looking for patterns in the large quantity of data you've collected during your exploration of **What *is***. As you approach the conclusion of this stage, you've got some interesting data and are ready to begin separating what is important from what is not, looking for patterns and insights that will give you a new window onto reality. The goal is to establish the criteria for the **What *if*** idea generation stage, which comes next. To accomplish that, you must organize and present your data in a way that lets hidden patterns and implications emerge. And you need to engage your collaborators in this process to create a common "mind" among them about the desired qualities of the designs you will create together. Note that in using the term *mind mapping* we are not referring to a particular kind of diagram (a "mind map" or a "spider diagram," for instance). Instead, we use the term to describe the process of extracting meaning from a vast amount of information.

When to use it: You move into mind mapping when you feel like you have collected representative data from each key constituent—customers, suppliers, partners, and your own operations—and are eager to begin generating ideas. Since you will always want more information, the shift from data collection to mind mapping is often driven by the project schedule more than by confidence that you have collected all the information you need. The knowledge that you are not searching for a single right answer helps you let go of the need for certainty in the mind mapping process.

Why mind mapping de-risks your growth project: The early tools in the **What *is*** stage yield a sea of data. The first challenge is processing all this information so that you can actually *use* it to generate better ideas than you would have otherwise. The second equally important challenge is aligning the organization around the ideas you choose to advance. Not meeting these challenges—learning nothing from the data or disagreeing on the most promising ideas they suggest—is a prime source of waste and failure in growth projects. Mind mapping helps you avoid both pitfalls. With it, you are trying to replace the "business as usual" culture of debate about the one right answer with a focus on exploration and dialogue—while remaining data-driven. Mind mapping builds a common mind about current reality and thus decreases people's allegiance to the solutions they had going in to the project. That is why mind mapping must be a team sport.

For many people, mind mapping is the most difficult part of the design process. No smoker came out and told Pfizer that he or she viewed the habit as a lifestyle choice rather than a medical problem. That insight emerged as the team pored over its information, looking for patterns. Ultimately, these led to the aha! moment and the reframing of the business. But it was hard work getting there. There's a lot more art than science to mind mapping. It is easy to become overwhelmed—in fact, this stage is often an emotional low point. And intuition plays a big role, so it is ambiguous and hard to structure.

This is where your "inner detective" comes into play. Think of yourself as Sherlock Holmes at the scene of the crime, surrounded by potential clues, trying to assemble them into a coherent story. Like Holmes—and Watson—you're paying particular attention to what *doesn't* fit (like workarounds or pain points), the kind of red flags that are always missed by the bumbling inspectors dispatched by Scotland Yard.

Mind mapping calls for the kind of creative leap that can be uncomfortable for those of us who have been trained analytically. Fortunately, we humans tend to be pretty good at pattern recognition. Eons of experience have trained our minds in this way; we've been trying to turn our brains into calculators for just a few hundred years.

Getting Started

1. **Hold a yard sale.** Mind mapping begins with laying out the data you've collected for everybody to see. This can be a daunting task. Traditionally, managers produce reports summarizing their learning, which they expect their teams to read and analyze before they come together to discuss their next moves. That approach may be sufficient for truly dedicated and diligent teams working together on a continuous basis, but we have found that relying on intensive advance preparation from a large group, such as you'll want to invite to mind mapping, leaves a lot to chance. Months of exploration often produce voluminous amounts of information that can overwhelm those not intimately involved with the project, and so careful attention to the presentation of data is crucial for engaging those who have to date been outsiders.

Our suggestion is to lay out all the data in a yard sale (or an art gallery, if that metaphor works better for you). To do this, you are going to tap into the power of visualization to display the key components of what you've learned as clearly and simply as possible. Chances are you already have some customer journey maps, persona 2x2s, and value chains to display. That's where you begin. And then you probably want to make posters that capture key themes and trends from both these and your secondary data. (Note: Copy stores can make a large black-and-white poster-sized copy of a PowerPoint or Word document very inexpensively.)

Let's return to the Darden team to look at its mind mapping process. As members of the team continued their work to identify opportunities to enhance the MBA experience, they realized the importance of involving faculty and staff in looking for insights and patterns and imagining new possibilities. Their challenge was centering these discussions on the data they had collected rather than letting them become opinion sessions, during which a tired set of pet ideas would be rehashed. In the exploration phase, team members had journey mapped the experience of students, recruiters, faculty, and staff; conducted focus groups with students, alumni, and advisory groups; examined reports on the state and future of higher education; and studied demographic and business trends. Those invited to the mind mapping session would have neither the time nor the inclination to read the hundreds of pages of reports they had prepared.

Their solution was to create a gallery of data. They made inexpensive posters of key summary slides from each report—large enough to read from a short distance—and hung them in a little-used hallway along with personas, journey maps, the team's original charter, and the school's mission statement. They organized the gallery according to stakeholder group and included short quotes made by faculty and staff members during the various meetings and pictures of students and faculty at work together. Aside from some concerns from the custodial crew about the effect of the tape on the freshly painted walls, the team was pleased with the look of the gallery. (They compromised with maintenance by using special tape.)

2. **Invite shoppers.** Tell a group of thoughtful people—anywhere from ten to 50—that you want to borrow their intuition for a day or even just an afternoon. When they arrive, assign them to seats at small "team" circles. Each person needs a marker and two stacks of medium-sized Post-it notes in two different colors, one stack of large (5x8) Post-its, and a clipboard.

> More than 50 Darden faculty and staff attended the mind mapping event. They had been asked to organize themselves into teams beforehand and arrive ready to get to work. Each was handed a clipboard with a reminder of the innovation team's charter on one side and a schedule for the session on the other, along with a stack of Post-it notes and a marker.

3. **Offer tours.** Kick off the event by asking your guests to tour the yard sale (or art gallery). Depending on their familiarity with the process, you may need to spend some time (but not too much) moving around the room explaining briefly what each visual describes.

> Starting at different parts of the gallery, Darden team members gave a 15-minute gallery overview tour.

4. **Pick out the good stuff.** Ask attendees to browse individually (without talking to one another) and note (on separate medium-sized Post-it notes) any learnings that he or she believes should inform new ideas. Each person will probably generate 20 to 30 of these. If important data are missing from the gallery, attendees can add their own, but on different colored Post-it notes. (Have teams start in different places around the room and ask everyone to write in large box letters.)

> To the Darden team's amazement, faculty followed instructions, working in silence for a full 20 minutes. That experience alone created a unique memory.

5. **Cluster the good stuff.** Have attendees return to their circles and spend five minutes privately sorting through their Post-its and clustering them into themes, using their clipboards. After completing this, each team should work as a group to cluster members' combined Post-its into shared patterns and themes on a large foam-core board. We suggest the following approach:

One individual offers a theme that seems significant and attaches his or her relevant Post-it notes to the board. The other team members then add to that cluster their own relevant notes.

A second person then offers another theme. The process is repeated as before, with participants adding to this second cluster their own related Post-its. The group continues in this way until all major themes have been gathered on the board.

At the conclusion, any Post-it notes that have not been assigned to a theme are posted in the margins as "outliers." Pay attention to these: Just because a piece of information doesn't fit into a cluster doesn't mean that it isn't important.

> Most teams got off to a slow start. But as team members began to present their Post-it notes to one another and use them to create clusters, conversations became animated. The resulting boards were not pretty, but they were very meaningful to the groups that created them.

6. **Identify the insights** related to each cluster and look for connections between clusters. Ask the teams to step back and try to identify what insights arise from each cluster. These should be written on the large Post-its and posted on top of the relevant cluster. Teams should then look for relationships between the clusters.

7. **Translate insights and connections into design criteria.** Pose the question, "Based on what you have learned, if anything were possible our design would…" Capture these criteria on a flip chart, one per team.

>One of the Darden teams produced the following criteria:

>*"If anything were possible, our design would … "*

>*deliver a differentiated, meaningful experience to students and recruiters that is uniquely Darden and consistent with our mission statement.*

>*create an end-to end experience from admissions through graduation that is powerful, coherent, and integrated across functional disciplines and curricular and co-curricular.*

>*allow faculty members to each get to know 100 students as well as we now know the ones in our small intensive courses.*

>*articulate the educational outcomes we are really serious about and talk explicitly about how we achieve them.*

>*deploy more of Darden's attention and resources to building deep relationships with smaller recruiters in a process that feels customized to both the students and the recruiters.*

>*insist that faculty own the entire curriculum, not divide it up into separate fiefdoms and protect our own territory.*

>*support ongoing innovation AND experiment with game changers.*

8. **Create a common criteria list.** Have the teams browse one another's charts, discuss the criteria, and work together as a large group to create a "master list" of the criteria an ideal design would meet.

>When the design criteria generated by individual teams were compared across teams, a surprising (at least to faculty) degree of consensus emerged about the desired qualities for any new design.

Try This at Home

Go somewhere with rich visual evidence. Your well-decorated refrigerator is an ideal spot to practice mind mapping. Other spots in your home might be a cluttered pin-up board, an old desk that needs cleaning, a junk drawer, or a very full bookshelf. The only other things you need are a pen and a notepad.

This activity is designed to take about 30 minutes, but don't rush. At the end of the exercise, part of your home will be organized to suit your priorities and you will have learned to use a new design thinking muscle.

1. **List assumptions.** You have assumptions about what is most important on the refrigerator in the same way you will have assumptions about your customer and your field research.

    Some assumptions you may have in this case:

    - I already know what is on my refrigerator.
    - I already know what is most important on my refrigerator.
    - I already know what to throw away and should do that first.

    What if you do not know what is actually on your refrigerator (in the same way you can't hold all of your field research in your mind at once)?

    What if what you *think* is important is not what you *feel* is most important? Both logic and intuition are important in mind mapping.

    What if by looking at all the throwaway items *as a group,* you can establish a rule about what is allowed on the fridge in the first place? Insights can emerge even from data the manager of a research team initially thought was irrelevant.

2. **Make visual order from visual chaos.** Take everything down and lay it out on a table or on the floor in a neat way (but not according to any organizing principle).

3. **Compare and contrast.** Create clusters of items that are similar. Think broadly about your themes. You can cluster important phone numbers, family pictures, pictures of friends, to-do lists, and grocery lists. You can group things that are predominately blue or predominately red. Do not be afraid to move items from one group to another.

Are the themes of any of your clusters opposites? If so, move the clusters as groups into a pair of opposites. Perhaps you initially clustered all your magnets, but you could separate them into opposites: one group of functional magnets (with phone numbers for hospitals and pizza delivery) and another of decorative and humorous magnets.

As you go through your clusters, what do you learn by comparing and contrasting them? Jot down how these differences could be meaningful or useful to you. For instance, "When all my phone number magnets are together, it is easy for me to find them and to realize which important numbers are missing. Maybe my family shouldn't have to Google our primary care physician's phone number and address."

4. **Sort by the five Ws: Who, What, When, Where, and Why.** Look at your clusters. Most people initially create themes based on "What" or "Where." Feel free to tear your clusters apart and rearrange them according to "Who," "When," and "Why."

   Who:

   - Think about who gave you the items on your refrigerator and who put them there. Perhaps all those baby pictures should form a family tree?

   - Consider regrouping the items according to who in your household considers them most important. Would that make a useful organizational system?

   When:

   - In what order did these items arrive in your home? Do they form a to-do list that can be organized in order of urgency? In order of importance?

   - Is there a way to organize any of the items into a story that is meaningful to you?

   Why:

   - Which items are particularly important to you and why? You could create clusters to illustrate your pride in each child, to conjure up shared memories with your spouse, or to consolidate all of your take-out and delivery resources including menus, phone number magnets, and coupons.

Jot down thoughts on which of these organization schemes are most meaningful or useful to you.

5. **Reflect.** You should now have a notepad full of reflections of which organizational methods were the most useful (functional) and the most meaningful (emotional). Some may also have social benefits to you and other members of your household. You can now recreate the organizational method you found most useful on your refrigerator.

Of course, in business you don't have to limit yourself to one organizational method. As with other forms of data, it can be very useful to slice and dice the data, to organize and display the same data set in a variety of ways. Some organizing frameworks will help you make decisions, some will help you share what you have learned, some are high-level and abstract, and others can capture more detail. Coming up with different frameworks is a messy, iterative process. Any designer can tell you it looks a little different every time you do it. But it works. You now have the tools to create order from chaos.

Transitioning into What *If*?

As you prepare to enter the next stage of design, **What *if***, you need to distill your findings from mind mapping into an efficient form for use during idea generation. This is where project management aid 2, the **design criteria**, comes in. We can't overstate how crucial it is to establish design criteria *before* you begin generating solutions. To reverse this order is to tempt people to bias the criteria to favor the solutions they like instead of those that best meet customers' needs. If you take the time to establish clear design criteria before you move to the next stage, your team will have a shared sense of what makes for a superior design. The design criteria provide a yardstick for how you will judge designs, yet they are not a blueprint for any *specific* design.

Imagine you are 11 years old and your goal is to earn $100 to buy a new bicycle. You decide to set up a lemonade stand at your community pool, and you believe it will take more than one day to reach your earnings goal. The design criteria for your lemonade stand might look like this:

- Transportable in the trunk of dad's car
- Weatherproof in case of rain
- Provides shade
- Flat surface for pouring lemonade
- Tall enough for a cooler to sit below
- Durable enough to be reused several times
- Costs less than $10
- Must be completed by Friday evening

None of these elements tells you exactly *how* to design the lemonade stand, yet they eliminate certain choices (watercolor paints are out, for example) and guide other choices (a table seems prudent). If you give these criteria to a designer, he or she will be happy. It's clear how you will judge their work, yet there is room for them to discover an innovative solution.

These are the type of criteria we will need for the **What *if*** stage. Having successfully applied the first four tools in your new design tool kit, you are ready to move from talking about current reality to creating a new future.

SECTION III:
What *if*?

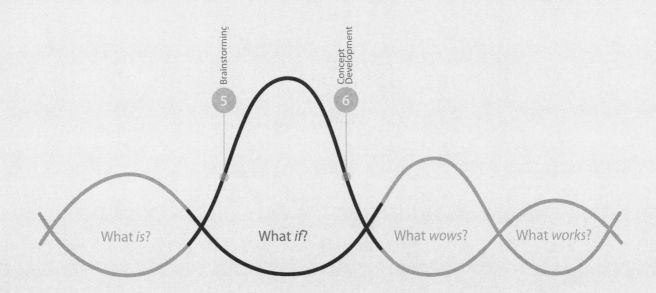

Brainstorming

5

Concept Development

6

What *is?*   What *if?*   What *wows?*   What *works?*

Meet Mark Stein, another accountant and management consultant turned design thinker. But Mark doesn't warm to the label "design thinker." "I'm just a good problem solver," he says. "I get hooked easily with a good business problem. It becomes like a puzzle, and I try to think of every possible way to approach it." Mark views his undergraduate degree in business, five years in public accounting, and four in management consulting as good preparation for becoming an entrepreneur: "My public accounting training and consulting experience are an advantage in a couple of ways. First, I love the details, and I always believe there is wisdom and truth in them. I look at the tiniest details and find things all the time. I also have a practical eye for all the moving parts required to make a new concept work."

The puzzle that caught Mark's attention in 1999 was the shortcomings—and attendant growth opportunities—associated with the rise of Internet shopping. Mark and some colleagues thought that there was money to be made in creating software to improve the consumer's experience. So they launched a start-up, which they named Brivo Systems, and immersed themselves in an investigation of shoppers' current e-commerce experience. They identified a few "pain points" that seemed to be calling out for software solutions:

- Finding rarely bought items was not easy (in 1999, Google had been around for less than a year).

- Qualifying for group discounts on e-commerce purchases, as a single buyer, was not possible.

- Buying repeat items, such as regular household consumables, was more trouble than it should have been.

- Working couples often could not be home to accept deliveries. In fact, Mark's team discovered, a residential delivery required an average of 2.2 attempts—the so-called last-mile problem.

The Brivo Systems team emerged from its exploration stage with a broad design challenge: facilitate consumer e-commerce through a hosted software application that would address some of the pain points listed above while meeting the start-up's business objectives. Particularly interesting to Mark and his colleagues was the challenge of dual-career couples who wanted to shop online for household consumables, such as toothpaste and paper towels, but were not home when the delivery truck came by.

The Brivo team also had some ideas about the criteria for a solution: It had to be easy for customers to use, scalable, and Internet-based. It had to be secure and protect deliveries from theft or vandalism. It needed to create network effects that would allow it to go viral (maybe by rewarding users for enrolling others). On the business side, an ideal solution would position Brivo deep in the e-commerce information stream and generate the kind of data that shippers, deliverers, and receivers would come to rely on. The Brivo team wanted to be fast to market (show proof-of-concept within six months) and to stay out of the hardware business (to avoid capital cost and timing risks).

Using those criteria, Mark and his team held a series of brainstorming sessions to frame some possible solutions. They invited both insiders and external experts, including the head of operations for Peapod (the online grocery service), the director of marketing at Intuit (the creator of home software for financial management), the operator of a dry cleaning business that did home delivery, and the president of a courier service.

Three weeks of brainstorming resulted in a range of ideas. On the software side, these included demand aggregation software that would help groups of people get discounts and resupply software to help households manage low-value consumables. On the last-mile problem, ideas included an opt-in neighbor holding system; a network of local pick-up spots, such as a 7-11 store; a residential "smart" mailbox connected to the Internet; a bank of smart mailboxes in high-density residential settings (similar to lockers at a ski area); and a weatherproof, cable-reinforced secure bag that a delivery driver could hang on a door handle (the empty bag could then be mailed back or picked up during the driver's next trip into the neighborhood).

From these ideas, the Brivo team developed three concepts for further exploration: the Consumulator (software that would let groups of people aggregate their demand and qualify for volume discounts), the Cuckoo Click (software that would help consumers arrange regular deliveries of household items), and Oscar the Smartbox (a smart mailbox, or "smartbox," that could accept deliveries, named for the Sesame Street character who lives in a garbage can).

The Brivo Systems story moves us to the next stage. Now that you have thoroughly explored and documented **What** *is*, you can look toward the future: **What** *if*. What if you could help people locate hard-to-find items or get great discounts? What if you could make the "Sorry We Missed You Note" obsolete?

If you think this sounds a bit like brainstorming, you are right. The **What** *if* stage is inherently creative and generative, but it must go well beyond simplistic expressions of new possibilities (the kind of output that a brainstorming session might produce) and arrive at robust concepts that can be evaluated, prototyped, and (if promising enough) developed. The topic of brainstorming alone is the subject of many books. However, it is not necessary to

Design Goal	Brivo will create a scalable, Internet-based software solution for one of the following customer pain points: 1. Finding rare items to purchase online is not easy. 2. Qualifying for group discounts on e-commerce purchases, as a single buyer, is not possible. 3. Buying repeat items, such as regular household consumables, is more trouble than it should be. 4. Working couples cannot be home to receive deliveries; a residential delivery requires an average of 2.2 attempts.
User Perceptions	• Easy to use • Secure and trusted
Physical Attributes	Any device designed to solve pain point 4 must be: • Theft-proof • Weatherproof • Large enough to receive a shoebox-sized item • Relatively easy to install and maintain
Functional Attributes	• Must make e-commerce easier for users • Should make e-commerce easier for another stakeholder, e.g., retailers or delivery services • Must position Brivo in the e-commerce information stream and generate useful data for shippers, delivery agencies, and users • Should create network effects that would allow it to go viral (maybe by rewarding users for enrolling others)
Constraints	• A proof-of-concept model must be possible within 6 months. • Any solution must be positioned in a way that helps the existing ecosystem of e-commerce delivery rather than directly competing with it or hindering it.

*All statements, numbers, and timelines within this document are the supposition of the authors and do not reflect the actual design criteria used within Brivo.

be an expert at brainstorming to be successful at design thinking; brainstorming is merely a stepping stone on the way to developing concepts.

This is when you take a creative leap, and most businesspeople dread it. But we have good news for you: If you are more architect than artist, there's cause for celebration. This process depends more on structured protocols than on pure leaps of imagination. As Larry Keeley of Doblin advised us:

> *"Creating new concepts depends a lot more on discipline than on creativity. You take the ten most creative people you can find anywhere. Give me a squad of ten marines and the right protocols, and I promise we'll out-innovate you."*

One of the disciplines that Larry and his squad of Marines know is the discipline of stepping away from traditional critical reasoning, which breaks down ideas and finds the flaws in them instead of building them up into something new. We are trained in this kind of thinking throughout our academic and business lives—it is often our strongest professional habit. But part of asking "What if?" involves putting that skill on hold and exploring a wide range of possibilities. Successful design thinkers use clever mental tools and tricks to get out of the habit of breaking things down. One especially powerful category of such tricks is metaphors and analogies.

Using metaphors does not require a new muscle. How many times have you said, "Sorry I didn't get back to you. I had to put out a fire"? All we're asking you to do here is to use a metaphor or an analogy to imagine a future possibility. For instance, in its effort to reinvigorate Nicorette, the team at Pfizer based its brainstorming on the idea that a smoking cessation solution could be similar to a gym membership. Team members came up with this analogy after discovering, during the **What *is*** stage, that younger smokers don't view their habit as a medical problem but as a lifestyle choice. Asking how trying to quit smoking could be like joining a gym freed them from the habit of looking for the weak link in any proposal. Instead, they took leaps of imagination and formed a story that included a personal coach, a social support system, and a scale where people "weigh in" to see the declining level of toxins in their systems (each of those features made it into the final offering, in one form or another).

Christi Zuber offered another example of the power of analogous thinking, drawing from her group's efforts at Kaiser to reduce medication errors. As part of the exploration process, the Kaiser team identified companies in other industries that struggled with the issue of reducing errors in critical situations. Team members visited those

MAKE USE OF METAPHORS

When we come up with metaphors, we engage in a deeply creative process—that of recognizing a connection between two seemingly unrelated things. As Linda Verlee Williams argues in *Teaching for the Two-Sided Mind*, the metaphor is a trick of language perfectly designed to share an open thought process with others and to communicate a deeper set of relationships and possibilities than appear on the surface.[1] The team at e-commerce software company Brivo Systems sometimes described its smart mailbox, which could accept residential deliveries if no one was home, as a "virtual doorman." This metaphor opened up new possibilities for uses (neighbors could drop off the key in their smart box) and provided inspiration for the web interface.

firms for what they called an "analogous observation," bringing along seven or eight Kaiser patient safety officers, managers, and patients. One visit in particular helped the team look at the issue in new ways:

> *"We went to a flight school and had a flight instructor go through how they do their checklists. He told us about the 'sterile cockpit': there should be no other conversations during takeoff and landing except those things that are about safety. When we debriefed what our people had learned from this analogous observation, they were really intrigued by that. So during our brainstorming session, we had them brainstorm ideas around that. As a result, we've changed the flooring around our medication dispensing machines to show these as 'red zones': when you're in these areas, this is our sterile cockpit."*

Bingo! A simple analogy is sometimes all it takes to set your inner critic on the sidelines long enough to imagine an exciting future. The **What if** stage makes use of other cognitive tricks, too, from personas to trigger questions to contra-logic to a chili table (you heard us).

Tools in This Section

The **What** *if* stage includes the **brainstorming** and **concept development** tools. It ends with our third project management aid, the **napkin pitch**, which helps you summarize the main attributes of your concepts and start working with them. Brainstorming (and its trendier synonym, ideation) causes many businesspeople to recoil. Trust us, you can do this. We share Larry Keeley's confidence that the results depend more on disciplined execution than on blue-sky creativity. The key is to approach brainstorming the right way and couple it with concept development to translate your ideas into concrete, fully developed concepts.

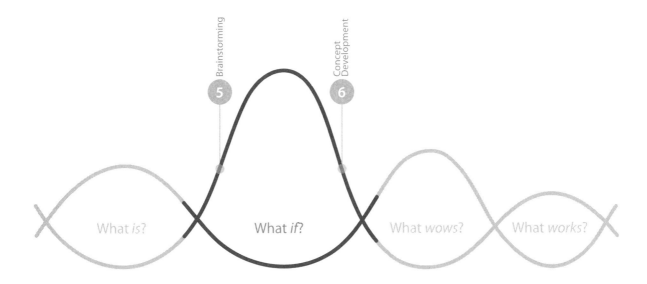

FOUR REASONS PEOPLE HATE BRAINSTORMING

There was a time when people looked forward to participating in brainstorming sessions. Today, the bloom is off the brainstorming rose, and little wonder why: Nearly every manager has been involved in failed brainstorming, where you go to an off-site location, play with squishy balls, are entertained by an external facilitator with little grounding in your business, create a zillion Post-it notes, and end the day in a room cluttered with debris and with no follow-up process in place. Here are four reasons people hate this type of brainstorming, along with our solutions to create sessions people will love—because they improve the future of the business.

1. **Problems are poorly framed:** There are two kinds of people in brainstorms: the extroverts who shout out ideas no matter how irrelevant and the introverts who wish they could be somewhere else. Both kinds of people struggle when challenged merely to "think outside the box."

   Solution: Don't invite people to think outside the box. Instead, give them a clearly defined box by framing the challenge through user research and then providing good trigger questions.

2. **The usual suspects say the usual things:** Instead of bringing the strongest, most diverse team into a brainstorm, many project leaders invite large numbers of people for political reasons. Everyone brings their pet projects into the session and uses the time to justify them. The social extroverts take over despite the best efforts of the external facilitator. Result: Nothing is said that we haven't heard before.

   Solution: Keep the group small (12 people at most) and diverse.

3. **Brainstorms turn into critiques:** Most brainstorming sessions lack ground rules, so it is very easy for these sessions to turn critical instead of productive. After all, our inner critic is used to having a front row seat in business meetings.

   Solution: Set ground rules (such as, "Withhold judgment"). Enforce them quickly and without exception.

4. **Brainstorming makes more work, and the organization is going to kill all these ideas anyway:** Often there is no follow-up process for a brainstorm. And if there is, there is little reward for trying something innovative and a great penalty for advocating anything difficult and improbable.

   Solution: Don't conduct brainstorming unless there is a financial commitment to explore current reality, a team in place to develop alternative futures, and a sponsor with a track record of courage to see the project through.

CHAPTER SEVEN:
BRAINSTORMING

Brainstorming is the goal-oriented cousin of daydreaming; it is a way to generate ideas—in our case, fresh alternatives to the status quo. Brainstorming is so fundamental to how we think about innovation that you may be surprised to find so many activities in the design thinking process before we get to brainstorming. In fact, as you developed your journey map and did your value chain analysis, you probably noticed you were already coming up with new ideas. You almost can't help yourself.

When to use it: Use brainstorming at the beginning of the **What *if*** stage. The risk is using it too soon, before you have studied **What *is***. Many failed innovation projects skip **What *is*** and begin with brainstorming, only to fizzle out immediately. The resulting ideas languish in a vacuum, with no mind mapping to represent customers' true priorities and no design criteria to judge those ideas and galvanize a shared commitment to the best ones. Another risk is to pay only lip service (or less) to brainstorming. All too often business managers, confident in their ability to take action, rush into execution with the most readily available solution without having brainstormed at all.

Why brainstorming de-risks your growth project: This one is pretty obvious: You can't have innovation without new ideas. Brainstorming ensures that you consider ideas that can result in something fundamentally new in terms of value creation. It is your hedge against the risk of incremental thinking. This is an exciting phase in the design thinking process. You brainstorm in teams and groups so that you can harness the power of diverse viewpoints and experiences and tap into the group's collective intelligence.

This tool will teach you brainstorming as a discipline, a repeatable process you can use to trigger creative thoughts with high potential to create new value. The process will take the handful of new thoughts in your head and multiply them exponentially by incorporating new people, new perspectives, and new stimuli. Successful brainstorming should help you create many possible alternatives, from which you'll select only a few for further development.

A successful brainstorming process is like a fireworks display. People gather on blankets next to strangers. There are lulls and then bursts. Bursts seem to beget other bursts. And when the sun comes up the next day, there appears to be a mess to clean up. In the mess that's left after a good brainstorming session are the raw materials for several innovative concepts. In concept development, the next tool, your job will be to cluster and assemble the bits and pieces into a coherent form, all the while guided by the design criteria you established at the end of **What *is***.

Getting Started

Fireworks provide a high-energy, stimulating experience for the audience, but in the back of our minds we know the display reflects careful design. The same is true for brainstorming. Think of brainstorming as 90 percent planning and 10 percent execution.

The Zen of Brainstorming

More than 2,500 years ago, the Buddha taught his followers Right Thought, Right Speech, Right Action. Let's adapt that model to design thinking:

- Right people (small group, diverse and depoliticized)
- Right challenge (the design brief)
- Right mind-set (build up, not tear down)
- Right empathy (customer persona)
- Right inspiration (insights from journey mapping)
- Right stimulus (trigger questions)
- Right facilitation (pacing, individual and group tasks)
- Right follow-up (clustering and concept formation)

1. **Right People.** Success in brainstorming comes from using small, diverse groups, as free as possible from internal political considerations. Brainstorming cannot abide groupthink, so it is essential to go way beyond the project's core team. For many people, participation in brainstorming may be their only exposure to the project

(other than a status report down the road). If there are people you wish to involve purely to garner their support for the project at a later stage, then add a brainstorming activity especially for them rather than holding a megabrainstorm. Twelve people is a practical maximum size, and the group will probably need to break into smaller groups for some portion of a half-day or full-day session. Cross-functional groups can also be critical to success. But you can go further: What about inviting some outsiders to the sessions? Customers, perhaps? Or, even better, an impartial third party? The team at Brivo included several outsiders. But don't let the party get out of hand. In our experience, several sessions with smaller groups will be more valuable than a single large session.

2. **Right Challenge.** The brainstorming team must focus on a clearly stated challenge. The design criteria represent a great starting point. Often it will be helpful to include key elements of the design brief, too. These project management aids will tell participants everything they must know to be successful contributors.

3. **Right Mind-Set.** The mind-set you need for brainstorming is that of the creator, not the critic. To help people embrace the notion of building up instead of tearing down, you might start with an inspirational setting (off-site?), a springboard story (a previous success?), or even a galvanizing video (a customer expressing her problem in human terms?). In every case, you need to frame the discussions with a set of ground rules, such as:

- One voice at a time
- No filibusters (30 seconds per idea)
- Show your work (sketches and stick figures)
- Withhold judgment (evaluation occurs later)
- Build on the ideas of others
- Have fun!

> A recent one-day brainstorm for a digital photography team at Hewlett-Packard, charged with designing new digital photography experiences for mothers with young children, began with a challenge from the sponsoring executive, delivered over the phone like Charlie in *Charlie's Angels*. He asked the team to have the courage to include concepts that were certain to be criticized by others, and he included a "courage factor" in the evaluation criteria. That permission from the senior executive became a reference point during the day. The team worked all day and concluded with a briefing to the executive sponsor by web meeting.

4. **Right Empathy.** People are inspired by *people*. It's as simple as that. For a successful brainstorming session, participants must care about the problem, and that means that you must show them its human costs. Here is where

the fieldwork you completed in the **What *is*** stage can come in handy. Use it to create a persona of a customer who experiences the problem you are focused on. A persona, which we have talked about as a visualization tool, is not a demographic group. It is an individual, with a name, age, and concrete likes and dislikes.

> The team at Hewlett-Packard focused on "Jill," a 36-year-old soccer mom with two kids and too little time to get everything done. Session leaders described her to the brainstorming participants and explained her journey, including her pain points.

5. **Right Stimulus.** If there is a single attribute that makes or breaks a brainstorming session, it is the questions used to elicit new ideas from participants. We call these "trigger questions." Preparing a brainstorming session involves preparing a portfolio of trigger questions, framed in a constructive sequence. Rather than representing out-of-the-box or blue-sky challenges, a good trigger question defines the box you are playing in and focuses attention on a specific aspect. Let's say Brivo Systems was brainstorming about the challenge of dual-career couples wanting to use e-commerce to manage their resupply of household consumables like toothpaste and paper towels. Consider three possible trigger questions:

   1. How would household consumables be managed in paradise?
   2. How is resupply managed in mission-critical environments such as combat and mountain climbing?
   3. What if household items could be bought only at 60-day intervals?

The first question is a classic free-your-mind, blue-sky question. It's okay as a warm-up, but it tends to generate impractical responses. The second and third questions may appear too limiting by themselves, but as part of a portfolio of trigger questions they can be very effective. A successful brainstorming activity requires multiple trigger questions. Here are some keys to developing effective ones:

Use catalyzing quotes and stories. Verbatim quotes provide great stimulus to brainstorming groups. When Brivo team members set out to solve the problem of the last-mile of e-commerce delivery, they met a customer whose package had been left under the hood of his grill to keep it out of the rain. Forgetting the note the delivery person had left about the unusual delivery location, he fired up his grill a week later only to lift the lid and discover his new hiking boots "well done." The photograph he took and that story ended up on the wall in Brivo's brainstorming room.

Question your assumptions. We all have unarticulated assumptions about how things are done in our business. Unexamined and unquestioned, they can be the greatest impediments to seeing new opportunities. One approach to recognizing these mental "rules" is to lay out how our business operates today. Your value chain analysis should help you do this. How do your offerings move *physically* to the market? How does *information* flow? What about how the *financials* play out? Then challenge yourself to come up with one alternative scenario for each. Sometimes it pays to play the devil's advocate. Consider Barry Sternlicht, who, as CEO of Starwood Hotels, had an itch to explore all-white bedcovers even though everyone in the hospitality industry relied on floral prints in dark hues, believing that they hid signs of wear and tear and dirt. Former Starwood chief creative officer Scott Williams explained how Barry's contrarian approach helped the company develop its Heavenly Bed concept:

> *"Barry is a branding genius and had the persistence to keep asking everyone involved with the development of the bed, Why? Why should it be done as it's always been done? Ultimately, we gave it a try and discovered it is actually easier to clean white bedcovers because you can use bleach. Focusing on the bed and the linens was a game changer, as crazy as that sounds. Our guest satisfaction scores skyrocketed. It took Marriott nearly six years to follow our lead. When they did, Bill Marriott said, 'I've been in the hospitality business all my life, and I can't believe it took Barry Sternlicht to teach me how to make a bed!'"*

Explore the extremes. Extreme scenarios can often trigger novel thoughts. Imagine where Kodak might be today if, back in 1996, it had seriously explored the trigger question, "What offerings will we provide if 90 percent of the market shifts to digital photography?" If you are in the business of providing health care, ask, "What if we could be paid for this service only on the basis of health outcomes?"

Change who does what. Many of the most successful innovations come from shifting key roles in the value chain. EBay gets its sellers to "store" the inventory. IKEA gets the customer to assemble furniture. Online banking turns you into your own teller. Boutique hotels *become* the entertainment, instead of merely housing you in close proximity to the entertainment. To explore the notion of shifting roles, include trigger questions such as, "How could we offload (difficult task X) to another party?"

Explore technology scenarios and trends. Most markets are undergoing technology-driven changes. A good trigger question to explore this could be, "How can we let customers do self-service?" Another set of questions

CONTRA-LOGIC AND THE FINE DINING INDUSTRY

One of our favorite ways to trigger new insights is to invite brainstorm participants to act as contrarians. But instead of asking them to contradict everything, we focus their attention on the underlying elements that make the current business work. We call these the "dominant logic" of the business. For example, imagine you are a recent graduate of the Culinary Institute of America and you're looking for an innovative way to provide high-end gastronomical experiences. We could define the dominant logic of the fine dining market like this, according to the flow of goods, information, and money:

	DOMINANT LOGIC	CONTRA-LOGIC
Physical Flows	1. Fresh food from nearby markets 2. Seasonal ingredients 3. Location: High-end retail storefront 4. Food prepared to order 5. Mostly low-wage workers 6. Food consumed on-premises	1. 2. 3. 4. 5. 6.
Information Flows	7. Customers read reviews 8. Advertise in regional magazines 9. 60% reservations, 40% walk-in 10. Food management software	7. 8. 9. 10.
Financial Flows	11. Pay for food supplies daily 12. Customers pay after dining	11. 12.

Rather than try to upset all flows at once, we might ask a brainstorming team to focus on changing one or two to see what new combinations are possible. For example, if we change Physical Flow 3 to "Airstream trailer," we have a new experience where the food can travel to customers willing to try a high-end dining experience outside their building or even at their favorite National Park. This eliminates a high-cost element of the traditional business model—real estate—and opens up amazing possibilities. If we change Physical Flow 6 to "Food frozen and eaten at a later date," we have created a prepared-meals business model. Finally, if we change Physical Flow 5 to "Recently released prisoners seeking to build new life skills," we have DC Central Kitchen, a widely emulated community-development model that also provides great food.

can come from the top trends affecting your markets. If you are in a consumer market, a good trigger question might be, "How can we let customers configure and personalize our service?"

Pretend to be somebody else. Imagine that you are someone in an industry quite different from yours. As you strive to address an unfamiliar opportunity, ask yourself, **What** *if* …

- your firm was Apple and could find partners to orchestrate a seamless platform experience?
- your firm was Google and had a mission to empower the world with the ability to find information as quickly and easily as possible?
- your firm was Virgin and was by nature fun, irreverent, youthful, and engaging?
- your firm was Disney and saw all customers as guests to be treated royally?
- your firm was Wal-Mart and wanted to share savings with customers to keep them coming back for more?
- your firm was Harrah's and could anticipate and respond to the exact moment a customer was ready to walk out of the casino?

Stand in the future and back-cast. Finally, some people will find it easier to imagine an alternative future if you place them in that future and ask how they got there. We call this back-casting. It leverages the powerful notion popularized by Stephen Covey, which we mentioned in Chapter 3, that one should start with the end in mind. Brivo could stimulate new possibilities through a back-casting question such as, "Amazon wants to offer our solution as a shipping option. What attributes did our solution demonstrate to earn this opportunity?"

6. **Right Facilitation.** The key considerations are to build confidence, maintain pacing, and vary individual and group tasks. One of the most powerful facilitation mechanisms for group problem solving is a practice that Stan Gryskiewicz (cofounder of the Center for Creative Leadership) calls the "blue card."[2] It involves presenting everyone in the group with the same trigger question and inviting each person to *work silently* and write down at least three ideas on blue cards, one idea per card. You allow about three minutes for a round of writing, and then each card is shared with the group and posted for others to see.

 The first round tends to dredge up a bunch of ideas you have kicked around for years, so it's crucial to have a second round with the same trigger question, which one of our colleagues calls the "echo round." This gives participants the opportunity to reflect on what they heard and build on it, often by combining two different notes on the board in a novel way. This exercise makes it impossible for one vociferous extrovert to dominate the group and ensures that everyone is engaged. It also builds the group's confidence in itself and in the brainstorming process. (Note: This method has been proven to generate *three times* as many unique ideas as facilitated oral brainstorming, even after eliminating redundancies.)

Small-group activities are valuable, especially after participants have established themselves through some blue card rounds. Competition can also get the creative juices flowing. For example, if you are brainstorming about an online experience for managing a chronic disease, you might divide a 12-person group into three teams and give each team the same trigger question: "How can this experience take advantage of the mobile phone?" Have one team focus on the tech-savvy patient, one on the tech-average patient, and one on the tech-laggard.

A final consideration is pacing: You have to keep it fresh for participants. If they have used the blue cards for three rounds, change the approach to facilitated oral brainstorming on a flip chart. Alternatively, you can assign people to different teams, which will unleash new energy. Or you can move outdoors for the next session. Mental exhaustion will come at some point, but resourceful facilitation can keep it at bay and help produce something truly novel.

7. **Right Follow-Up.** Brainstorming sessions can fall victim to two errors. The first is the mischaracterization of the output as "concepts." In fact, the output of brainstorming is ideas that have the potential to be combined into coherent, compelling new concepts. If you try to evaluate the ideas in their raw state, you will almost always find them lacking. There are too many unknowns, too many unstated assumptions. The process that converts raw ideas into robust concepts that can be evaluated is described in tool 6, concept development. This is best done by a small team and can occur in the days that follow the conclusion of the brainstorming sessions. The second error is neglecting to set aside resources and methods to convert the results into an implemented solution. Tools 7 through 10 overcome this and help the most compelling concepts find their way into the world and create value.

Try This at Home

Professional development and education sometimes get pushed to the back burner. Why not try a design thinking approach to your own professional development in the coming year? Conduct a brainstorming process using these steps:

1. Set a goal for how you want to use a modest budget (time and travel funds) to create a professional development experience that will provide significant benefits to you, your supervisor, and your subordinates; convert this into a design brief.

2. For some context, document your professional development for the past five years. What development experiences have you had? How much effort did they require? What benefits accrued to you and others? What were the emotional high points and low points for you? Keep this brief—a maximum of three flip chart sheets.

3. Prepare at least six trigger questions to fuel a proper brainstorming session. Include contrarian questions such as, "What could I *teach* others that would help me develop?"

4. Invite one or two people to help you brainstorm about your professional development (they can be a coworker, a mentor, and even your spouse).

5. Do the brainstorming formally (if it helps, you can talk about yourself in the third person). Be sure to provide ground rules, and use the blue card process for at least three rounds. Don't stop until you have at least 50 ideas on cards or Post-it notes.

6. Now, look at the results. Did your trigger questions work? Are some surprising ideas on the board?

    Note: Save your ideas—we will use them for the "Try This at Home" exercise in the next tool, concept development.

CHAPTER EIGHT:
CONCEPT DEVELOPMENT

Concept development is the act of choosing the best ideas from brainstorming, assembling them into detailed solutions, and then evaluating those using both customer and business criteria. It is analogous to what the movie director does back in the studio, editing the good bits into something creative yet coherent. Whereas brainstorming is best done by a diverse group that includes people outside the innovation project, concept development requires a dedicated core team: Outsiders often lack the context for the project as well as the time it takes to perform concept development.

You want to build *multiple* concepts so that you can offer a choice to your audience, the customer. If you come up with 200 ideas during brainstorming, you might use them to create 12 concepts, from which you will test three with customers and ultimately deploy perhaps just one.

When to use it: Use concept development immediately after brainstorming (as part of the **What *if*** stage). But make sure you have pushed yourself to create a wide variety of novel alternatives and are truly ready to zero in on the few best ones. Concept development gets you ready to evaluate your concepts against the design criteria.

Why concept development de-risks your growth project: The output of brainstorming is nearly always too raw and incomplete to be evaluated using the design criteria. The concept development process takes the most innovative ideas from brainstorming, combines them cleverly, and completes them with business logic. Ultimately, this phase is crucial both to protect novel ideas from being pruned too early and to prevent you from getting so caught up in the excitement of value creation that you neglect to address the business case for your new idea.

Getting Started

Have you ever built something out of Legos? Concept development is a lot like that, except you want to build several "somethings." To understand how this works, let's consider a challenge facing a division of Siemens and see how it used the results of a brainstorming session to develop some interesting concepts.

In 2003, Siemens Building Automation was experiencing steady sales growth but declining customer satisfaction ratings. The problem, the division discovered, was something called "ad hoc requests," a client's request for a minor modification. Two types of Siemens staff worked with clients: around 2,000 service technicians, who found the idea of "selling" repugnant and preferred to avoid interacting with the management team at the client's site, and approximately 200 account executives (in North America), who were busy writing new orders (which earned them commissions!) and were letting the ad hoc requests fall through the cracks. Siemens needed a way to solve the ad hoc problem without crippling its sales growth.

The Siemens service quality team studied the context, framed the problem, and generated several dozen ideas through a brainstorming activity. The ideas included forming SWAT teams to go from facility to facility to do ad hoc repairs; recording all ad hoc requests electronically and managing them centrally; letting the client write the proposal through pre-formatted ad hoc requests; providing a 72-hour ad hoc closeout guarantee; programming the service technicians' handheld devices to produce automatic proposals; using local contractors in lieu of Siemens technicians; and instituting a "frequent fixer" program to reward technicians who closed out ad hocs quickly.

1. **Gather your Legos.** First, assemble the key ingredients you will need for concept development: a core team of people, the design criteria, and the brainstorm results.

2. **Spread out your Legos,** similar to the yard sale we created in mind mapping (Tool 4). It is easier to work with a hundred or more ideas if you can see them easily and move them around. We like to put everything up on the walls as if we were in an art gallery. Leave extra space so you can move items as you see relationships and patterns. Begin to organize the ideas using the following methods:

- Eliminate redundancies
- Put similar ideas next to each other
- See what is missing and add ideas where possible
- Make a list of themes that emerge, such as

  - Self-service
  - Pay as you go
  - Personalization

  - Direct to consumer channel
  - Staging / pre-service
  - De-featured solutions

- Set priorities using the design criteria
- Put stars on the must-have ideas and themes

> Mark Hadding at Siemens recalls reviewing the brainstorm results. None of the ideas struck him and his colleagues as a bolt of genius. None of them even represented a complete, coherent solution; they were merely elements that could help, if they were combined in the right way. As Mark explained: "We weren't really discouraged, but we weren't sure how to proceed, either. There were some intriguing pieces to work with. Finally, I realized we needed to have a brainstorm *after* the brainstorm, but this one would focus on creating some interesting combinations."

3. **Choose some anchors.** Choose five to 12 themes to serve as anchors for distinct concepts. If you are working on ideas for smoking cessation, as the team at Pfizer was, you might try to build concepts using anchors such as buddy system, cohort of strangers, phone coaching, contest, guarantees, and feedback systems. The team at Siemens generated concepts around several anchors:

   - Account executive productivity tools
   - Customer self-service
   - Incentive schemes

   - Third-party services
   - Service technicians engagement

4. **Form initial concepts (make some chili).** Finally, you are ready to form some concepts. This step draws from the principles of architecture. You will be combining different elements from the brainstorming, but you want them to be thematically connected, balanced, and proportional, and they should form distinctive concepts. The

fancy term designers use for this phase is "combinatorial play"; it has to do with picking and choosing elements that combine to create both compelling customer value *and* a viable business model. In this case, the whole is often greater than the sum of the parts. In concept development, clever combinations trump the lone "killer idea" every time.

One of our favorite approaches to combining ideas in interesting ways was taught to us by Jeremy Alexis, a professor at the Illinois Institute of Technology, whom we met in Chapter 1. He encourages his students to set up a "chili table." Here's how it goes:

- Think of all the categories of things you can put into chili: meat, beans, veggies, spices, etc. (Jeremy calls these his "variables")

- Now think of all the possible items in each category, such as different kinds of meat and spices (Jeremy calls these his "values")

- Now create different combinations of variables and values to make different kinds of chili. You might make vegetarian chili (lots of veggies, no meat), meat lover's chili (every kind of meat, no veggies), or Hawaiian chili (ham and pineapple, hold the cayenne pepper). You get the idea.

Jeremy's chili table is a nifty metaphor for unleashing new combinations, which is exactly what the team at Siemens did:

The service quality team "made some chili" and came up with a range of solutions, including:

- Account executive special bonuses and productivity tools for fulfilling ad hocs

- Reward Store: An all-volunteer loyalty program for service technicians to execute ad hoc repairs without involving account executives

The Reward Store concept took best advantage of the existing human capital: There were ten times as many service technicians as account executives. To overcome the technicians' dislike of selling, Siemens presented Reward Store as a "problem-solving service" (technicians love to solve technical problems). This concept also included an automated proposal tool (another idea that came out of brainstorming), which further diminished technicians' sense that they were selling services, and the opt-in structure gave them a choice in the matter. After some refining of the Reward Store concept, Siemens implemented it. In the first six months, nearly 50 percent of the service technicians registered for the program (which provided gifts from a catalog as the incentive), and customer satisfaction scores rebounded quickly.

The individual ideas that came out of Siemens's brainstorming might not have seemed very innovative. Building an application for the handheld device to generate automatic time-and-materials proposals didn't seem revolutionary. However, in the context of the behavioral problem it solved (keeping the service technicians from feeling like they were selling) and in the way it was combined with another idea (the reward points system), it became novel and compelling. Ultimately, clever combinations of little ideas are often what turn growth projects into winners.

Most important, the solution uncovered by Siemens is rooted in the observations the team made during the ethnographic research it had conducted in the **What *is*** stage. Successful growth projects are rarely the result of random brainstorming magic; they emerge from a disciplined application of design thinking that is rooted in users' unmet needs.

Try This at Home

At the end of the brainstorming tool, we did an exercise to brainstorm ways to transform your own professional development process for the coming year. Now let's use the results to perform concept development. Here's the exercise:

1. **Assemble your Legos.** Gather your design criteria and the results of the brainstorm. Optional: Invite one of your brainstorm companions to help with this part, too.

2. **Spread them out.** Put the design criteria on the wall, along with the results of the brainstorming session. Organize the ideas, make a list of themes, and choose at least five (and no more than ten) ideas or themes that seem essential to meet the design criteria.

3. **Choose some anchors.** Choose at least three (and no more than five) themes to serve as anchors from which to build professional development concepts. Go for diversity and excitement. These themes should excite you as the potential customer and your supervisor, as well.

DEVELOPING THE COVER OF THIS BOOK

To provide a simple example of brainstorming and concept development, consider the cover of this book. It was created using the design thinking process. Back in late June 2010, Jeanne said to Tim, "Give some thought to what should be on the cover." Before heading to Charlottesville for a working session, Tim mocked up a simple cover showing the word "Growth" with a bare lightbulb hanging where the "o" should be, shining down on a petri dish with a sprout rising out of it to seek the light.

❝ I love it," said Jeanne. "That's our cover!"

❝ Jeanne, you can't love it yet. We haven't studied any alternatives," Tim said. "A single choice is not a choice. Let's use the design process."

❝ Uhhhhhhh, all right," Jeanne agreed, wanting to be done with it but sensing she was going to have to walk the walk, so to speak.

During the drive back from Charlottesville, Tim brainstormed with his colleague Jenny Lynn Cargiuolo. They discussed possible covers using a variety of trigger questions, including:

- What are your favorite book covers and why?
- What says "Growth" to you?
- What says "Tools" to you?
- What says "Design Thinking" to you?
- What design style does this book need to have?
- What kind of cover will be approachable yet challenging for a manager?

From this discussion, Jenny Lynn sketched 18 alternatives in a notebook as Tim drove. Back in their offices, Tim and Jenny did a search of similarly themed books to see what type of cover designs they used. The goal was to be distinctive yet approachable within the category. This comparison process provided some dos and don'ts, which Jenny Lynn used to develop rough mock-ups of the 18 alternatives (a process that took less than two hours).

This was our brainstorming output; now we were ready for concept development. We looked at the 18 mock-ups and sorted them into five themes: growing plants, sketches that become real, tool metaphors, clever icons, and ingredients or patterns. We wanted to provide Jeanne and her colleagues at Darden with the best concept from each of those five thematic areas. Ultimately, we knew we would choose a single cover, and it might even combine elements of two different concepts, but the goal of the initial five concepts was to solicit some good feedback. After choosing our favorites, we mocked them up a bit better and laid in the title and subtitle, choosing appropriate typefaces and framing each one in a square format to match the page size.

Jeanne and three colleagues from the Darden School served as the "customers" of these covers, giving feedback in three quick rounds of reviews and enhancements. Not surprisingly, the petri dish cover did not make the first cut. The lightbulb was just too tired to carry another book into the market, our reviewers felt. Valid point, and no insult to the designers. Within days we arrived at the design that informed the cover of this book. Total processing time: approximately 14 hours.

4. **Form initial concepts.** Pick an anchor and start tacking on the ideas that seem relevant to it. Do the same with the other anchors. Don't worry about using some of the ideas in multiple concepts, as long as each concept looks distinct from the others.

5. **Fill in the details.** Complete the exercise by following this template:

   - What type of education/development experience am I considering? How would it work?
   - What key development needs does this meet for me? How does it benefit my supervisor and colleagues?
   - What are the costs and risks?
   - How would it enrich the compact between the firm and me?

Transitioning to What *wows*?

As we transition from the heady creativity of the **What *if*** stage into the sobering reality of **What *wows***, where we'll need to make some tough choices about what to do next, we'll use another project management aid—the **napkin pitch**—to elaborate on each of the concepts we've generated. The napkin pitch is not to be confused with the elevator pitch: what you say about your project during a two-minute elevator ride. The napkin pitch has a little more breathing room, and its role is to express each concept in a way that makes it easy to compare them.

The corporate innovation unit at financial services company The Hartford, officially called White Stag: Innovation at The Hartford, is among a growing number of groups that use a version of the napkin pitch. White Stag's format, adapted from Silicon Valley R&D organization SRI International, is called NABC, in reference to the four quadrants of the napkin, each of which is devoted to answering one of four strategic questions:

- Need: What is the unmet need we are addressing?
- Approach: What is our approach to meeting that need, and how is it novel?
- Benefit: How does the customer benefit? How do we benefit?
- Competition: What competition will we face, and what advantage will we have?

It is inevitable that the innovation process will demand a tough choice among high-potential projects. That's okay—napkins that were finalists in Q1 can always be introduced again, when additional resources become available. The use of a standard template enables comparisons as your experience grows.

At The Hartford, as at other organizations that use the tools of design thinking, what's important is to avoid becoming committed to one concept at this stage of the innovation process. With multiple compelling concepts to explore, the greater the odds that you'll find one that just might be in the "wow" zone.

What *wows?*

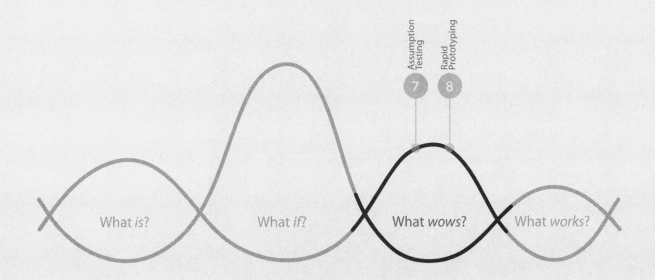

Assumption
Testing

Rapid
Prototyping

7   8

What *is*?   What *if*?   What *wows*?   What *works*?

Remember Diane Ty at AARP and Project Prepare for the under-50 financially challenged? Diane and her team moved through the **What *if*** stage, brainstorming and then creating a number of different concepts for a new website—all under the banner of "helping people of all ages make smarter choices today for a better life tomorrow."

Two of the concepts are captured in the following napkin pitches. The first was built around the idea of a lending community for debt repayment. The idea was to give Gen Y members (and others) a boost so that they could manage debt and begin to develop savings habits. AARP would facilitate this by providing contract templates, interactive tools, and payment plans to its members and those to whom members provide financial support.

NAPKIN PITCH: Lending Community for Debt Repayment

Need

Debt Management

Gen Y customers with student loans:

- Feel dread of being "alone with debt forever," which can create apathy toward debt management
- May not understand how to prioritize payment of different types of debt (i.e., credit card debt vs. student loans vs. home loans)
- Parents/relatives have difficulty collecting money when they make informal loans to "help out"
- Face a downward spiral of debt

Approach

AARP provides contract templates, payment plans, and/ or billing mechanism.

- AARP could help its members formalize their approach to providing money to their adult children
- AARP could provide flexible templates for contracts and payment plans (and recommendations for how to best leverage them)
- AARP could work with a partner to provide a no-cost or low-cost formal billing mechanism

Benefit

- Gen Y users gain a "new lease on life" by getting out from under the treadmill of servicing student debt
- Gen Y users can still learn responsible debt repayment but at significantly lower interest rates
- Parents/relatives have a formal contract that is agreed to for loan repayment
- Parents/relatives can still "help out" financially, without interfering with growth of financial independence and responsibility

Other Service Providers*

- Circle-lending platforms
- Traditional loan servicers
- Lawyers
- Informal community lending

*This quadrant would generally be labeled "Competition," but nonprofit organizations do not technically have competitors.

The second concept focused on life planning through various visualization tools, such as professional guidance provided by volunteer financial experts, interactive financial resources, and an ongoing community discussion.

NAPKIN PITCH: Life Plan Visualization

Need

Life Planning

Gen Y customers in the Overwhelmed, Catastrophic, Optimistic, and Achieving segments ALL:

- Face important life decisions
- Struggle to visualize the impact of financial decisions on their lifestyle and lifestyle decisions on their finances
- Struggle to weigh the importance of different demands on their finances

Approach

A virtual reality where users can visualize various lifestyle trajectories and get advice on life stage decisions. Possible features could include:

- A lifestyle and life event simulation tool
- Narrative component to explain common pitfalls and offer advice
- Highly graphical, highly interactive visualization that aggregates multiple financially complex decisions into a simple, approachable diagram
- Inspirational & Individual: "Write Your Own Adventure" or "Your American Dream"
- Fun: "Game of Life" or "Second Life" world where avatars encounter life stages
- AARP 50+ members serve as online mentors
- Financial experts provide pro bono advice

Benefit

- Gen Y users are freed to pursue their "Dream" by allaying fears associated with dramatic life changes
- Gen Y users can receive personal guidance from experienced advisors who have "been there, done that"
- AARP 50+ members may find it rewarding to serve as community mentors

Other Service Providers*

- For-profit, in-person financial advisors
- For-profit, phone-based financial advisors (e.g., Charles Schwab)
- Financial diagnostic quizzes offered by financial institutions (e.g., USAA)
- Newspaper and online advice columnists

*This quadrant would generally be labeled "Competition," but nonprofit organizations do not technically have competitors.

Napkin pitches in hand, the AARP team identified 40 different assumptions underlying the concepts that needed to be tested before they could go any further. Diane explained:

> *"We laid out our hypotheses and then through this iterative process started knocking away at them, using not only original research but also research reports or even news articles and looking at evidence to either support or refute the hypotheses along the way. Where there was a disparity, we would say, well, how are we going to resolve this? And then it would either inform a next activity for prototyping or in some cases would lead to the decision that we needed to spend the money to do original research again."*

One of the key assumptions was that an offering that was endorsed by AARP would be more powerful than a standalone brand. The team carefully documented the evidence it already had that supported or contradicted this assumption. For example, the team had conducted research indicating that AARP was regarded across generations as a trustworthy, credible advocate for older people. Members and their families said this linkage would make them feel more favorably toward a new offering. Earlier research by AARP, however, suggested that the organization's image conflicted with the concept of services for young people. And third-party data on new brands that had established instant credibility with the younger adult set, like MySpace and Facebook, questioned the value of established brands in this market.

AARP team members decided that they needed a market test to resolve the issue. They moved into action, deciding to prototype and test four approaches to Life Plan Visualization (napkin pitch 2), each with a different level of association with the parent organization: The first made full use of the AARP brand, the second used the AARP logo and the tag line "helping people of all ages make smarter choices today for a better life tomorrow," the third contained a reference to AARP only in the About Us section, and the fourth featured videos of users talking about the new offering and AARP's sponsorship of it.

Let's step back and consider what Diane and her team are up to now. They have completed the first two phases of design thinking. Through the exploration of **What *is*,** they have learned a great deal about the lives of the young people they hope to serve. Through brainstorming and concept development in **What *if*,** they have homed in on some concepts that they believe have real potential to create value for their intended customers and meet organizational objectives. Now it is time to make hard choices, identifying the best concepts—those that *wow*—in order to guide further investment decisions. To do this, the team needs a clear-eyed view of the key assumptions that must hold true for the concepts to succeed and a plan for testing them, either using data they've already got or going out and getting new data from customers.

To determine **What *wows*,** you must test the future in the present—a tricky business. But we do it all the time. When you test-drive a new car, when you hold a suit in front of yourself and look in a mirror, and when you write a preliminary agenda for a meeting, you are testing future possibilities without leaving the present.

Unearthing key assumptions (and then subjecting them to tests) is the emphasis in the **What *wows*** stage. You will first test these assumptions, to the extent possible, in *thought* experiments. After exhausting this approach, you will then test any remaining assumptions through *physical* experiments, conducted in the marketplace, in which actual customers interact with a prototype of your new offering.

A thought experiment, like a physical experiment, starts out with a clearly stated hypothesis and uses data to determine whether it is likely true or not. Unlike a physical experiment, however, which involves moving into the marketplace and *acting*, a thought experiment uses logic and existing data in a mental process that involves only *thinking*. And so thought experiments look more like the analytics that we normally do in business.

Physical experiments, on the other hand, necessitate finding an efficient means to express the new concepts to others so that they can help us in the assumption testing process. Because mental experiments (which use existing data) are usually more economical to conduct than physical ones (which involve going out and getting new data), we try to do as much assumption testing as possible using thought experiments.

Of course, our hypotheses about the future can never be tested directly *until* we move into the marketplace (the topic of Section V, Chapters 11 and 12). Without doing that, the only place you can look for evidence is the past. Yet under conditions of uncertainty, data from the past don't have much predictive power. Deciding when you can safely use data from the past and when you can't involves using a process that historians Richard Neustadt and Ernest May have called "thinking in time":

"Thinking in time has three components. One is recognition that the future has no place to come from but the past; hence, the past has predictive value. Another element is recognition that what matters for the future in the present is departures from the past, alterations, changes, which prospectively or actually divert familiar flows from accustomed channels … A third component is continuous comparison, an almost constant oscillation from the present to future to past and back, heedful of prospective change, concerned to expedite, limit, guide, counter, or accept it as the fruits of such comparison suggest."[1]

Thinking in time is the iterative process that Diane described above. If it seems a bit like solving a simultaneous equation, that's because it is. Typically, the *wow* zone for a business concept occurs at the intersection of three criteria: Customers have to want it, the firm has to be able to produce and deliver it, and doing so has to allow the organization to achieve its business objectives. For Siemens Building Automation, the Reward Store solution (which we described in Chapter 8) sat at that intersection. And it was compelling because it solved the problem of customers' ad hoc repair requests while leveraging the division's most abundant asset: the service technician. However, the participation of service technicians also represented a key assumption that needed to be tested.

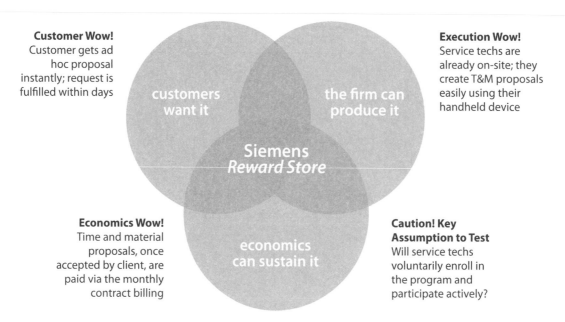

Customer Wow!
Customer gets ad hoc proposal instantly; request is fulfilled within days

customers want it

the firm can produce it

Execution Wow!
Service techs are already on-site; they create T&M proposals easily using their handheld device

Siemens
Reward Store

Economics Wow!
Time and material proposals, once accepted by client, are paid via the monthly contract billing

economics can sustain it

Caution! Key Assumption to Test
Will service techs voluntarily enroll in the program and participate actively?

Tools in This Section

The two tools in this section begin to transform your napkin pitch concepts into actual marketable offerings. **Assumption testing** identifies and begins to test, using thought experiments, key assumptions upon which a concept's success hinges. **Rapid prototyping** works to express a proposed concept in the most efficient form for further exploration, testing, and refinement.

These tools reflect a balance between focusing on what's missing (insight into the key assumptions and what we don't know) and what's present (embodied in the prototype). Of course, the two must inform each other en route to figuring out **What** *wows*. As you read these chapters, observe the interaction between what you know and what you don't know. This goes to the heart of the kind of uncertainty you need to pay attention to when designing for growth.

The overarching goal of **What** *wows* is to express new concepts in ways that showcase the amazing elements while you iterate to improve the weaker ones. And we want to remind you again that the life of a growth project is far less linear than the lineup of our tools suggests. Especially in this stage, assumption testing, prototyping, and even customer co-creation (which we've placed in the next stage, **What** *works*, but could just as easily occur as part of **What** *wows* or even **What** *if*) interact in an iterative dance as we use what we learn to refine our concepts.

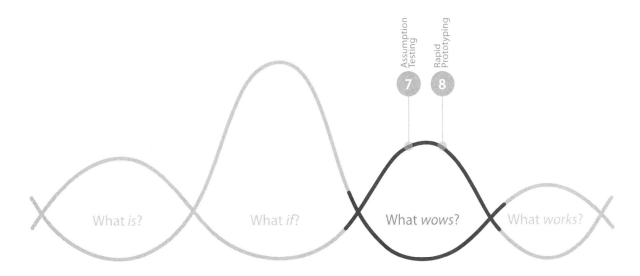

CHAPTER NINE:

ASSUMPTION TESTING

Assumption testing is a tool for surfacing the key assumptions underlying the attractiveness of a new business concept and using data to assess the likelihood that these assumptions are true. The approach acknowledges that any new business concept is actually a *hypothesis*: a well-informed guess about what customers desire and what they will value. Like any hypothesis, a new business concept is built on some assumptions about what makes it attractive. Those assumptions must be valid in order for the hypothesis to be "true." And so testing them is essential. If, for instance, our hypothesized value proposition rests on the assumption that customers really care about (and will pay a premium for) convenience, we had better find out as quickly as possible if that is in fact true.

The first step here is to identify and articulate the assumptions. The second is to choose between two options for testing them: gather new data in a *field* experiment in the marketplace or use existing data to conduct an analytical *thought* experiment without going into the marketplace. Since marketplace experiments tend to be costly and visible, it's a good idea to conduct your first tests using data you already have.

When to use it: Assumption testing is an essential activity once you have a defined concept, which is why we introduce it in **What *wows*.** However, it can be a valuable technique much earlier in the process and later in **What *works*.** Many design thinking practitioners define their assumptions even before going into the field to do ethnography during **What *is*.** Surfacing your assumptions about customers and their preferences makes you more alert as an observer—and more cognizant of your biases. Later in the process, it helps you to prioritize; you usually have more interesting concepts to try out than you have resources available. Even given abundant resources, you don't want to market test anything you don't have to.

Why assumption testing de-risks your growth project: When growth projects fail, it is *always* because reality turns out to be different than you thought it would be: Perhaps customers don't want a new offering, your firm can't execute it, partners don't like it, or competitors copy it quickly. Launching new concepts to see if they sell is a risky and potentially expensive approach that you want to avoid for all but the most attractive ones. You minimize risk and expenditure by market testing only those concepts that pass a set of initial thought tests.

Assumption testing focuses on identifying the make-or-break elements of your concept. It involves taking a cold hard look at its key vulnerabilities. There are several common ones to look out for, including adoption rates, market entry timing, and availability of key partners. Mark Stein of Brivo Systems kept what he called a "red flags" list of the key vulnerabilities of the e-commerce software, which he updated throughout the process.

Think of yourself as an entrepreneur making a pitch to a venture capitalist. You don't know enough to *guarantee* success, but you must be supremely confident that you have selected a worthwhile problem, you have the foundations of a novel and compelling solution, and you have a clear view of the critical vulnerabilities and what it would take to test them.

The principles here are the same. Organic growth projects are about exploring unknown possibilities, and they require prudent decision making in the face of uncertainty. Since you aren't seeking risk capital from a professional investor, the job of this design thinking tool is to be a proxy for that investor—to help you focus on the critical elements on which your concept depends. So pay particular attention to levers that move the economics, like price, cost, and adoption rates.

Of course, no growth-minded manager wants to focus on the bad news. But the sooner you can find the fatal flaw in a new concept, the sooner you can either fix it with your inventiveness or move on to a more-promising concept.

Getting Started

It is time to drill down to the core assumptions on which the success of your proposed business concept depends. The steps in assumption testing are as follows:

1. **Lay out the *generic* business tests your new concept must "pass" in order to move forward.** At this stage, your goal is to see what it will take for your new idea to become an attractive, viable business, so you can use a set of tests that apply to just about any new business in any industry:

    1. The value test: Customers will buy it—at a price that works

2. The execution test: You can create and deliver it—at a cost that works

3. The scale test: If you pass 1 and 2, eventually (the sooner the better) you can build a level of volume that makes it worthwhile

4. The defensibility test: After you do all the work involved in steps 1 through 3, competitors can't easily copy you

Pretty simple. Think valuable, doable, scalable, and defensible. Those are the core issues involved in identifying and testing the attractiveness of any new business concept.

> Imagine that you are a newly appointed business development officer at a home loan company, recently acquired by a large credit card firm, and you have been given a mandate to identify and develop a growth initiative. Your new parent company is one of the largest credit card issuers in the United States, with more than 60 million accounts worldwide and a reputation as a leader in direct marketing and online services. Besides credit cards, the company offers a variety of financial services such as auto loans, small business loans, home equity loans, and second mortgages. It does not, however, offer first mortgages. Being new to the mortgage business, you immerse yourself for several months in the ins and outs of the industry and finally identify a number of growth opportunities that you believe have high potential. One of your favorites is a first mortgage product aimed at high-net-worth customers of the parent company, delivered with personal service through your bank branches. You believe that your proposed concept can pass all four of the tests:
>
> 1. Customers will value the convenience of personal attention from your bankers, one-stop shopping for all their financial needs, and the superior rates your knowledge of their credit history will allow you to offer them.
>
> 2. Your parent company's ability to deliver outstanding quality and fast turnaround time online for financial products is well known; you also already have bankers in your branches.
>
> 3. Historical data tell you that your parent organization has 35 million customers with excellent credit ratings.

4. Established competitors in the marketplace, like Bank of America and Wells Fargo, are busy cleaning up the mess in their subprime mortgage business, so you see an opportunity to enter without fear of retaliation on their part.

2. **Lay out the *specific* business tests your new concept must "pass" in order to move forward.** These relate to your firm and your particular situation. What are the important strategic goals you are trying to accomplish with this new concept? What assumptions are you making about how and why this concept accomplishes those goals? Refer to the first two project management aids: the design brief and the design criteria. The design brief should remind you of the strategic organizational goals you aspired to as you began the innovation journey. The design criteria will contain the imperatives that the business concept must meet, based on your customer ethnography and value chain assessments.

> Since one of the drivers behind the acquisition of your firm by the large credit card company was expected synergies between the two organizations, this new concept should be a great fit with strategic goals.

3. **Make sure that your assumptions relating to each individual test (value, execution, defensibility, and scalability) are as explicit as possible.** Remember that these assumptions revolve around a set of educated guesses you've made about the following:

- Customers: Why this concept will create superior value for them, how much they will be willing to pay, and whether there are enough of them to constitute a market of sufficient size.

> As you think more deeply about your concept, you realize that your value proposition rests on a number of important assumptions. One is that your high-net-worth customers value the face-to-face service your bankers can deliver.

- Your organization: How the organization will create and deliver the promised value and what capabilities it will leverage. You must also identify which critical capabilities are missing and whom you will partner with to obtain them.

> Although your parent organization's superb online capability is well established, your ability to deliver this new product also rests on the skills of your branch bankers. Do they have the

necessary skills? You also realize that you are assuming that your parent's scale in its Internet-driven credit card business will apply to scaling a personal service business.

- Competitors: Which competitors are likely to be affected and how they will react. This would include assumptions about whether and why they are capable of copying the concept quickly and how else they might interfere with your efforts.

    There are many competitors in the field, but you are assuming that they will not notice or respond to your entry into their business.

4. **Determine which assumptions are most critical to the attractiveness of your new concept.** If you've been thorough, you have probably generated far more assumptions than you can feasibly test. Can you highlight the handful that make or break your new idea? Timing is also important to consider. Generally, the two tests that matter most in the early stages of the innovation process are the value and execution tests. Scaling and defensibility come later, as you know more about the offering. Most new concepts fail the value test rather than the execution test, so that is where we suggest you focus initially.

    You decide that the value test is the place to start. If a significant proportion of your target high-net-worth customers does not value either the personal service you intend to provide or the convenience of one-stop shopping, your concept is unlikely to succeed.

5. **Having narrowed the assumptions down to a manageable number, you now must identify the data you need to test them.** It is crucial here to think through what the data look like that would either confirm or disprove your hypotheses. Given that managers are obsessed with data, you'd think this would be a piece of cake, but this task turns out to be surprisingly difficult. Most managers have been taught to take the information they've *got* and work with it. Here you are identifying the information you *need* and then figuring out how to get it. This takes practice and patience—and a team with a range of perspectives. Here is where the "designated doubters" come in handy. They are adept at looking for flaws in logic, whereas leaders of innovation tend to be hopeless optimists. You need both qualities to find and execute growth. This is where you figure out how to get the doubters on your team, sharing their concerns in a productive way.

One of your team members—always the doubting Thomas—brings up what he sees as a possible flaw in your logic: What if high-net-worth individuals have financial advisors who handle their important financial transactions, such as a new mortgage? They already have personal service and one-stop shopping; they don't need these features from their mortgage provider.

6. **Sort the data you need into one of the following three categories:** what you know, what you don't know and *can't*, and what you don't know but *could*.

Let's look at each category in turn:

1. **What you know.** These are the facts related to each assumption that are already in your possession. Beware of *beliefs* masquerading as facts. Don't confuse the two. The doubters will help you with this by highlighting the areas where your personal (and sometimes optimistic) interpretations may be blinding you to some realities that need to be acknowledged.

   You know quite a bit. For instance, you know that your parent company has a great capability set for doing financial transactions online and a lot of high-net-worth customers.

2. **What you don't know and *can't*.** This is the stuff that you can't know without a crystal ball. It is the land of true uncertainty, the land of the *unknowable*. No amount of experiments—either thought or real—can resolve this uncertainty. The only thing you can do here is predict.

   There are some larger macro issues that matter to your new concept's success—issues like housing starts and prime rate levels. You could make some predictions here, but you aren't sure how to test these, except against "expert" opinions.

3. **What you don't know but *could*.** In any situation, there is a lot of stuff that is knowable, but you haven't yet taken the time to go and get the data. Generally, this can be an expensive proposition, and you don't want to chase data that you don't need. That is why it is critical to take a hypothesis-driven approach, identifying only the really important data and then spending the effort to get them.

   Some of this information may already exist in your firm—or in the industry (or in another industry)—and you just need to go out and collect it. This is what strategy consulting firms do. But as we've already noted, it is hazardous to use data about the past (or even the present) to predict the future. In some cases, it is much better to make that future happen and then observe the results. For assumptions in this category, you can't get good data until you move into the marketplace. The learning launch (tool 10) will teach you how to conduct inexpensive, low-risk tests in the real world.

> You realize that there are a lot of customers out there, already in the parent's database, whose views about issues like convenience and personal service you should understand better. There is also probably some information floating around somewhere, maybe in HR, on the qualifications of bankers in your branches.

7. **Figure out how you could quickly get data in category 3** (what you don't know but could) that lends itself to thought experiments. This is where the fun begins. You are going to have to *construct* some data, which means not relying on what your internal accounting systems or industry trade group chooses to give you.

> You decide that determining how your target customers feel about personal service and value does not lend itself to a thought experiment. After all, they are already in the database, you know who they are, and they are reasonably inexpensive to reach. Why do a lot of analyses based on past data, which may not reflect what they really think, when you can easily just ask some of them? You decide to do a marketplace test, a learning launch, to improve your knowledge on the value proposition's attractiveness.

> You could also do a marketplace test on your branch bankers' skill set. This seems less necessary, though, because a thought experiment may be all you need here. You could spend a lot of time and money visiting branches to assess their skills, but you are reasonably sure you can find some data somewhere in-house—on training and certification, for instance—that can educate you on this subject.

8. **Design your thought experiment, paying special attention to the data that could prove you wrong.** How many times are we going to repeat this, you ask? No matter how often we do, it won't be enough. This is your Achilles' heel (and every other manager's as well). There is nothing you can do to reduce the risk of growth that is more powerful than paying close attention to signals that your assumptions may be wrong. Often these assumptions

are about how customers (and partners in your value chain) will behave—the traditional revenue data collected during pilots won't allow you to even test these. So the more explicit you can be about what those signals would look like, the better the chances that you will be on the alert for them—and that they will make it through your denial mechanisms. This kind of signal should be on a "red flags" list of the kind Brivo's Mark Stein kept.

Once your thought experiments are under way and you have started to refine your knowledge of the attractiveness of the new business concept, it is time to turn to the key assumptions that need to be tested with actual customers and, eventually, in the marketplace. This is the focus of the **What** *works* stage. To do this, you will need to create a prototype, the subject of our next tool.

Try This at Home

Assume you have the idea of creating a universal instructions portal, where instructions for every gadget, toy, game, tool, and what-have-you can be found. No longer would people be forced to dig through a cluttered drawer, searching for a product manual, when something goes wrong. They could just go to www.instructions.com (assume you own the url), where they could find any instructions they'd ever need. Is this a good business idea? Here's how you can find out:

1. Make a short list of what would have to be true for this to be a good business.

    - To help you create this list, consider how you would answer the top ten questions you would expect a VC to ask, such as:

        – How will you get the big players to give you their user instructions?
        – How many consumer visits do you expect?

2. The answers to those questions are your assumptions. Which three or four are most crucial to the business? Those are your *key* assumptions. One might be:

    - "We can acquire instructions from consumer appliance makers because their call centers and websites already have them available for download."

3. For each key assumption, list some cost-effective ways to test it, short of actually launching a market trial.

    - For example, try downloading instructions for some popular consumer technology items.

    - If you need to estimate the volume of consumer visits, start by finding a third-party estimate of the total number of consumer devices in use.

You may not be able to test all of your key assumptions, but you may discover existing sources of data that confirm or refute several of them. This gives you a running start in determining the attractiveness of the business, and it provides a clear focus for the next steps, including the learning launch (tool 10).

CHAPTER TEN:
RAPID PROTOTYPING

Rapid prototyping is the creation of visual (and sometimes experiential) manifestations of concepts. It is an iterative set of activities, done quickly, aimed at transforming the concepts generated in the **What** *if* stage into feasible, testable models. You build prototypes as the next step in the assumption testing you started with thought experiments, but now you're going live. In prototyping, you give your concepts detail, form, and nuance—you bring them to life. Larry Keeley of Doblin calls prototyping "faking a new business fast."

It is easy to prototype a new toothbrush, harder to prototype a new business model. But both projects have a need for rapid learning before you build hard tooling or commit to new IT investments. Early prototypes are often crude and unfinished in appearance, and they are supposed to be that way, to look like "works in progress." High-fidelity 2D prototypes are more developed, usually taking the form of storyboards, user scenarios, experience journeys, and business concept illustrations. Eventually, you will use 3D prototypes that are "built out" (in design language) working models that contain more features and details.

When to use it: Build prototypes early and often. You prototype to learn rather than to "test" a theoretically finished offering. You want the process to be simple and quick so that you can "make mistakes faster," identifying areas that can be improved while agreeing on those that are working. Sooner is better than later.

Why rapid prototyping de-risks your growth project: Prototyping uses an affordable loss calculation: What is learning worth? What amount can you afford to lose to learn something that your competitors don't know (even if you don't move the concept forward). It is all about minimizing the "I" part of ROI, which allows you to test many variations of concepts, bringing more of what designers call "optionality" into the design process. The cost of a simple 2D prototype could be as low as a pen and some paper. You can afford to do lots of 2D prototypes—and to prototype individual parts of a concept as well as the whole thing. By making abstract ideas *tangible* to potential partners and customers, you can better facilitate meaningful conversation and feedback about them. The purpose of prototyping is to create something quickly that can then be tested with users, refined, and socialized with a broader audience.

One of the most tangible differences between design thinking and business thinking is prototyping. Designers' passion for it borders on fanaticism. In a recent working session, one of our designers kept stacking up sketches while we worked on the problem. It quickly became obvious that she was prototyping in order to think.

As a manager, you are probably more adept at thinking without drawing or prototyping. But you are not adept at helping others see your thoughts. That is why you must prototype—to make your thoughts explicit so that others can grasp them quickly and share their thoughts with you. A good prototype can be 2D or 3D, it can take 60 seconds or 60 hours—but it always tells a story that invites other people into an experience.

Architects create blueprints and models, product designers build physical prototypes. Business prototypers, on the other hand, generally use visual or narrative approaches: images and stories. A design thinker at Swisscom told us, "Images help you clarify why you care, before you become consumed with how to build it." Prototypes can even include role-playing and skits. Today's computing power has given rise to a whole new set of prototyping approaches: video games and simulations. Some prototypes capture a concept in its entirety; others represent individual elements so that each can be tested separately.

In addition to taking different forms, prototypes are used in different ways at different stages of the design process. The evolution of Brivo Systems' Oscar the Smartbox provides a case in point. When we left off with Mark Stein and his team during **What *if*,** they had identified three promising concepts. During assumption testing, Oscar the Smartbox emerged as the front-runner, and the team immediately began prototyping to answer important questions about the device. Oscar graduated from a 2D hand-drawn prototype to a rough 3D physical prototype, and then to more-sophisticated 3D versions. Steve Van Till, the CEO of Brivo Systems, vividly remembers the first time he demonstrated the market test prototype at a VC pitch meeting:

"The first Oscar 3D prototype was actually an Igloo cooler with this hideous electronic brain and keypad bolted onto it. It used a cannibalized RIM (Blackberry) radio to connect to the Internet. That gave us confidence that our operating system would work, but it was too clunky and crude for a VC meeting. So we built a miniature version of Oscar with elegant, rounded lines, and we hooked up an external keypad. We took it to [blue chip VC] in New York and it looked great on the mahogany table in their conference room. The partner entered the access code on the keypad, and about 45 seconds later his Blackberry buzzed with an e-mail message from our operations center saying, 'Your Amazon.com order was just delivered.' Then we had him try the key code several more times, to make sure it would expire after a single use. Another message hit his Blackberry: 'The key code from your recent Amazon.com order was reentered three times, but it is only valid for a single use.' We watched him reading his Blackberry and saw the smile spread across his face. His head started to nod 'Yes.' The mini-Oscar was pure magic."

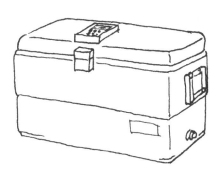

Early prototype

• Concept sketch (2D)
• Time to create: 5 minutes
• Materials cost: $1

Functional prototype

• Retrofitted cooler (3D)
• Magnetic door strike attached
• Keypad attached
• Time to create: 3 days
• Materials cost: $600

Market test prototype

• Original design by IDEO
• Fully functional
• Required original tooling
• Time to create: 3 months
• Materials cost: >$10,000
  (due to tooling cost)

Getting Started

1. **Start small and simple.** In our experience, nearly all firms build the sophisticated kind of 3D prototypes. Those are great to help you figure out *how* to build something, but at this stage we are more interested in figuring out *what* (if anything) to build. For that reason, the most successful growth projects prototype early and often. They permit their prototypes to feel unfinished. A prototype that leaves a little room for interpretation invites the user to contribute to it and complete it.

   Christi Zuber of Kaiser Permanente is a big fan of starting simply:

   "There's something magical about low-fidelity ways of trying something out. It automatically allows people to feel like they can put their fingerprint on it. The more polished, the more done up it is, the more people feel like it's already done. This is just a checkmark on your list of people that you need to run this through. They feel like you're not looking for feedback—you are looking for agreement."

2. **Figure out the story that you want to tell.** Visualize the concept in pictures, using as few words as possible. Add complexity, where appropriate, as you go.

   As Christi Zuber and her team at Kaiser tried to design a better way for nurses to administer medications, the story that evolved was about the best way to allow nurses to concentrate during this task. The story started with the images of nurses on roller skates we heard about earlier. This identified the problem. The story then needed a solution, which they discovered during a concept development session:

   "This nurse took an apron out of the prototype supplies and taped 'leave me alone' across the front of it. And they enacted this process where she was giving medications and people would come up and talk to her and she would point to the message on her apron. And we agreed that there was something intriguing about that. So we bought some cheap construction vests from Home Depot and gave them to a nurse and had her try it for one shift as she was giving medications."

   Nurses loved the lack of interruption—but not the Home Depot vests. So the Kaiser team created a reflective sash that nurses wear when they are giving out medications. The sash serves as

FORMS OF 2D PROTOTYPES

2D prototypes come in many forms, many of which will sound familiar:

Flowcharts: These are well known to managers with a background in process improvement. They represent a set of sequential activities, with arrows depicting the relationships among them. Journey maps are flowcharts, as are value chains. Use flowcharts to convey the basic building blocks of a new experience.

Storyboards: These can be simple sketches, or they can incorporate digital photos or screen shots. The sketch-based storyboard is familiar to anyone who has read a comic or seen a "making of" video for a feature film. Use this approach to move beyond the functional view and into the human story of the experience, to shift the focus to the user and the problem that the new experience solves in her life.

Metaphorical prototype: This could take the form of a poster with images that function as metaphors for a new service. For example, if you want to explore a two-hour solution to drafting a will, you might show an image of a pit crew working on a car that is stenciled with the words "Joe's Last Will & Testament." Use this to foster a gut reaction and promote a dialog with a target user, without doing any selling of specific features or benefits.

Videos: A video story combines elements of a storyboard and screen shots into a single format. The tutorials used by Netflix to familiarize people with its service were done as Flash demos, for example. Videos allow you to create the appearance of the service without actually building it.

Interactive building blocks: These are all about enlisting users in the design of a new experience and use a variety of approaches. One is the card-sort prototype, which presents the major elements (or building blocks) of the experience as a heading and invites users to design the elements under that heading by choosing pre-made cards. Card sorts are particularly useful for prototyping individual elements of a larger concept, allowing more effective learning about what combinations work for users (more on this in Chapter 11). Another format uses "pick and place," a storyboard that lets users arrive at forks in the road and choose a direction. We have seen this on wall posters and on computer screens. Even if the choices are not mutually exclusive, the decision points ask users to express their preferences.

Business concept illustrations: These are the most sophisticated 2D prototypes. Their aim is to express a new experience from multiple perspectives: the user experience, the technology, and the business model. They often seek to achieve high-fidelity finishes (such as brand positioning imagery, up to and including ad copy) to help audiences imagine that the experience already exists.

a visual cue that they're not to be interrupted. The prototype here is more than just the vest—it is the entire story surrounding it: who needs it, when, where, and why.

3. **Show, don't tell.** Make the prototype feel real through mock imagery and artifacts. Work on creating empathy—try to bring the observer *into* the concept. Focus on capturing details of how the concept will work and how people will experience it. Make the choices concrete. Use stories, maps, images, and movie trailers to spark conversation.

Christi Zuber told us another story to demonstrate the power of prototyping even if all you've got is sheets and paper clips. Kaiser was building a new medical office building designed so that physicians and medical assistants would work together in a shared space instead of having separate offices. Christi's team wanted to figure out how to prototype the space in a way that would be meaningful to the clinicians:

"We wanted to give caregivers an opportunity to provide feedback on our design without taking up a lot of their precious time. But showing them a drawing wasn't doing it—it just wasn't physical enough. A small-scale mock-up didn't fit the need either. So we took a conference room and mocked up the space by taking sheets, poking paper clips through the top of them, and then hanging them through the tiled ceilings. We measured out what the space size was that we thought might work, hung the sheets, got a cardboard box to represent the computer and an old patient bed from out of storage and put them in the room. We used other boxes where the sink would be and brought in clinicians. We just went up to their exam offices and asked them to come by the mock-up whenever they had the chance. They would show up and one of us would pretend to be the patient, and we would have them actually mock up an exam with us.

A lot changed from that exercise. We were a lot closer. And we were able to give staff exposure to trying it out so that their voice was heard. This is important. Trust is so much of this, and the more things feel like they happen in a back room, then I think the more chance you have of it failing, whether or not it is really a good idea."

4. **Visualize multiple options.** Create some choices to be made. Be willing to move the sheets.

> Christi continued her story of the examining room created from sheets and paper clips:

> *"Clinicians immediately knew what to do. They'd go over and pretend they were washing their hands at the sink. They'd pull up the chair. They'd sit next to us. They'd bring the computer over. They'd walk around and pretend to look in our ears. Then periodically we'd stop and say, 'How did that feel?' And they'd say, 'Well, actually, this space is a little too big. We thought we needed this much exam space, but it's a little too big. Things are a little far away, and I don't feel like I'm as efficient as I could be. I would actually rather the wall be a little closer.' And we'd stand up and take the paper clips out of that particular area and move it in six inches. And then we'd hop back on the exam table and say, 'Okay, let's do it again.'"*

5. **Play with your prototypes, don't defend them.** Let others validate them—not the people who created them. But always keep in mind what you are testing. Prototypes are about testing the assumptions you've identified as critical.

Try This at Home

Find a report that you rely on to do your job, but which you find especially hard to use. Print three copies of the first page. Now, try to imagine the report in some more usable formats:

- Format 1: Similar to what you have in front of you but with the most important bits color-coded—Green for "favorable" items that can be ignored, YELLOW for "caution," and RED for "broken" items that need your immediate attention.

- Format 2: Similar to what you have in front of you, but when you place your cursor over it, a dialog box pops up to tell you how that data point has changed recently and what corrective actions you have taken.

- Format 3: On the right-hand 2/3 of the computer screen is the information, and on the left-hand 1/3 of the screen is a video of a live person, describing the data as if he were providing the weather forecast.

Using a blank piece of paper for each format, create a low-fidelity prototype that you could show to your colleagues to get their feedback. Use parts of the printed-out page to make your job easier. Scribble or draw on it, no matter how humble your skills are.

Finally, find a person you can share the three ideas with and ask for feedback. Tell the person you are not committed to building any of the three prototypes—you just want his or her feedback. See how they react. Did they get it? Did they build on it? Do you think you would have gotten different feedback if you had merely explained the three alternatives orally or in text on a PowerPoint slide?

The idea is not to put all your best ideas into one version of the prototype. Instead, anchor each with a distinct element and build off the differences. Don't worry; you won't have to choose one. The ultimate solution could combine several of the best elements. The important thing is to try on different approaches, see what you learn, and notice how your mind changes during this process. You are prototyping to *think*, not to build.

Transitioning to What *works*?

Like our other transitions between stages, this one will be guided by a project management aid (our last one), the **learning guide**. This takes your conclusions from **What** *wows* and translates them into concrete guidance for achieving the crucial learning that will occur in **What** *works*—the stage during which you will engage actual customers to help you test your remaining assumptions, and do so with as little financial investment as possible.

The learning guide reminds us of the strategic intent and then highlights the key untested assumptions you must explore during your first experiments in the marketplace. It also defines the means you will use to test those assumptions and the financial capital you are willing to risk to do so. As you learn more through interactions with the customer during **What** *works*, you will update and clarify the learning guide.

In a venture-backed firm, the learning guide provides the underpinnings for each investment round. Though venture capitalists don't use this terminology, the typical VC firm provides just enough funding for a start-up to meet an important milestone of learning, usually a proof-of-concept with live customers. If the market response is positive, follow-on funding will be available. If not, the VC exits the investment but harvests the strategic knowledge of what worked and what didn't, which becomes knowledge capital that will inform future investment opportunities in their chosen markets.

Large enterprises have just as much to gain from learning opportunities in their markets. While the mechanisms for learning guides are often less formal in a corporate setting, the notion of learning as a driver of investment decisions is becoming more common. We see more and more corporations using protocols that are called return on learning, learning loops, learning contracts, or rapid results—all of which incorporate the principle of exchanging *financial* capital for *knowledge* capital.

Interestingly, the key problem that a learning guide addresses is not one of wasteful spending without realistic hopes of commercial success. Rather, the primary problem in a corporate environment is that development teams often play it safe to avoid "failure." Lem Lasher of CSC told us why his firm uses a form of learning guide:

> *"We gave up on the idea of finding people who are comfortable with failure. They don't come here. So in order to try risky things we had to redefine success. 'Find out if something is feasible or not,'*

we ask our project managers. 'Try to make it work, of course, but learning why it won't work is a form of success. Just do it fast.' And that framing allows us to get out of our comfort zone."

"Fail fast to succeed sooner" is the essential paradox of design thinking. The learning guide embraces that paradox by providing a mechanism to make sure your project isolates the most crucial lessons and learns them in an affordable way.

SECTION V:
What *works*?

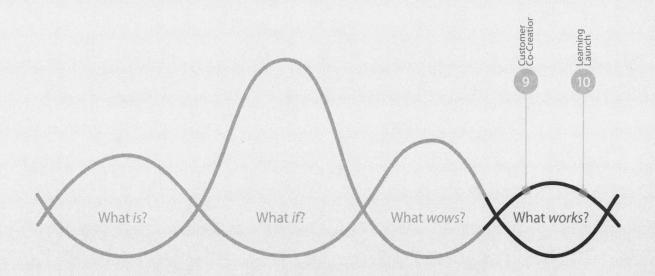

Customer Co-Creation
9

Learning Launch
10

What *is*?   What *if*?   What *wows*?   What *works*?

Our last phase of the design process takes us back to Dave Jarrett, the accounting partner we met in Chapter 1. No surprise—he is an expert on getting the most bang for your growth investment dollar. The key, to him, is involving customers in the process as early as possible:

> *"Our history before was we got a great idea, we built it, and then we went to the market and we tried to sell it. And you know what happens then—you get a lot of false starts. The analogy would be we'd let the engineers design the car. But they don't care about the looks; they only care about the mechanics, the technology. We're kind of like the engineers: We know how to build these solutions to address the industry need, but we need design or else we just deliver something that's not necessarily very pleasing to the buying public.*
>
> *What we do now is bring together a group of people who are focused on a particular area, and we'll go through a day or two process of trying to create a new opportunity that we could approach the market with, looking at things from different lenses and different ways. And then at the end of that we storyboard and take those concepts out to the potential clients, and we ask what they think about this proposed solution. I don't want to call it a cartoon, but that's kind of what it looks like."*

The "day or two process" Dave refers to results in a new concept, which gets translated into a learning guide. In order to explore the key assumptions, he and his Crowe Horwath team members create several concept storyboards. That's where customer feedback is the most crucial. Dave offers an example:

> *"We had a storyboard about an inventory management system that we wanted to do for car dealerships. We designed the storyboards around different color cars, and the cars were having a conversation. The red car said, 'You know, I don't need to know you guys very well, I won't be here long, because I'll sell fast.' And some other car said, 'I've been sitting here for a year and nobody cares.' We took that to a group of auto dealership CFOs and explained the concept to them. Then we passed the storyboard around the room and we asked them to put a green sticker on the concepts that made sense to them and a red sticker on the concepts that did not resonate with them. Then we just held it up in front of them and there was pretty good consensus among them of what aspects of this worked and made sense, what they would be interested in, and what aspects they had no interest in.*

Then we take that rough prototype, design the second level, and then go back again and say, 'Here's what we heard you say; here's another set of storyboards that kind of takes it a step or two further. Are we on track?'"

Getting his partners to go along with the design approach was not always easy:

"When we started, there were a lot of people who were not happy. They said, 'You're going to go out there, and you're going to sit down with these clients, and they're going to look at you like you're wasting their time on this.'"

It didn't help that the first group to go public with the approach was a coterie of bankers—both Crowe consultants and their clients. But to the amazement of all, the clients loved it:

"They ate it up. They were all in, having a blast. We planned an hour for these meetings. Every one of them was taking two hours. And the guys that took them out were bankers on our staff; they're not creative artists or anything."

Dave loves his client's enthusiasm for involvement, but the biggest payoff still comes down to dollars:

"The cost trade-off is astronomical, compared to what we used to do. We've got a few hours in these storyboards and some guys going out and meeting with their clients. Even if the idea goes nowhere, there is always value in meeting with your client. Plus the client always feels valued because you cared to ask what they thought. So there is never a down side to that. And we have saved ourselves a fortune, because in the old days we would have already built a $25,000 software prototype with no client input."

As Dave Jarrett demonstrates, figuring out how to move your most promising new concepts forward in the least expensive way isn't always straightforward. The preceding stage, **What** *wows,* can feel like the high point of the project from a design point of view. You have created a "wow" experience, checked the most crucial underlying assumptions, passed all four business viability tests, and expressed the concept in a prototype. Just look at it—isn't it beautiful?

LEARNING GUIDE	
We can imagine that Crowe's learning guide would have summarized the goals of the What *works* phase into something like the template below:*	
Strategic Intent	Introduce **inventory management software** for car dealerships that (a) lets a dealership easily identify slow-moving cars and price them according to their *true cost of carrying,* and (b) informs the dealership's future ordering process to minimize likely slow movers. The overall goal is to improve the dealership's per-car yield for an affordable one-time software investment and minimal ongoing maintenance cost.
Remaining Key Assumptions to Be Tested	• Dealership staff will enter data into the system within one day of a car's arrival on the lot with 99%+ compliance • The current sales incentive model can accommodate this new information in the workflow and create a win-win for management and salespeople

In-Market Test Plan

Untested Assumptions	Success Metric for Learning Launch
1. Dealership staff will enter data into the system within one day of a car's arrival on the lot with 99%+ compliance 2. The current sales incentive model can accommodate this new information in the workflow and create a win-win	• Dealership staff enter new-car data accurately within 36 hours of arrival for 95% of new cars arriving during 60-day trial period (to allow for learning curve) • Of 24 salespeople involved, 80% rate the system as either "good" or "excellent" • Same ratings from the six managers involved

Financial Capital to Be Expended	Learning launch of standalone software prototype for 60 days at two dealerships will require the following resources: • Learning launch manager + 1 support staff, both part-time on program • Not to exceed 200 hours of professional staff time • Software modification budget of 50 hours if necessary • Not to exceed $5,000 in out-of-pocket expenses for travel

*All statements, numbers, and timelines within this document are the supposition of the authors and do not reflect the actual learning guide used within Crowe Horwath.

It would be great if you could plant the flag right there and take a photo, but it is a false summit. There is another, steeper summit just ahead, where the exciting high-potential concept intersects with the marketplace. We call this fourth and final stage **What** *works*, and it represents the key difference between invention and innovation: *invention* is doing something in a novel way; *innovation* requires that the invention create economic value. Invention doesn't produce revenue growth or profit growth—only innovation does that.

Yes, your creations are beautiful; we understand the temptation to fall in love with them. But here's your dilemma: It's too expensive to keep all your options open and try everything. Yet when you develop just one concept, you are apt (as Crowe was in the old days) to leave a lot of money on the table when the customer is not interested in your masterpiece.

It is common practice for teams to envision multiple concepts and then choose one to move into market testing. The methods of choosing always have an air of analytic rigor about them—usually involving decision matrices or dot-voting schemes—but these approaches are fraught with biases. They open the door for team members to express their fears and aversion to risk, and what emerges is often a lowest-common-denominator concept, a safe bet that has little chance of igniting a customer's passions. You need to avoid this, and only one person can help you. It's the same person who inspired you to create those 300 Post-its in the first place: the customer.

Instead of observing some potential customers as they navigate the world of **What** *is*, you now need them to take a walk with you into several possible futures and to co-create a solution with you. This means putting your prototypes in their hands and refining them on the basis of their input until you arrive at a version that is ready for testing in the marketplace, using a tool we call the learning launch. This step of the journey will give us enough information to make solid data-based investment decisions. The **What** *works* stage, the culmination of the design thinking process, triggers a significant stream of communications, whether of victory in the market or lessons learned at an affordable cost.

If you are like a lot of managers, you will find **What** *works* to be closer to your comfort zone than a lot of the design-y work like brainstorming and prototyping. In many ways, this seems like running a pilot. But it isn't. You are not piloting a line extension for an existing product (exploiting known certainties); you are co-creating a new offering with customers (exploring unknown possibilities). This first contact between a new concept and the market is still a design work in process.

As you explore the tools in this section, remember that you may yet decide that none of the new offerings are feasible. This is when you find out, and you must retain your design thinking mind-set throughout—that is, you must stay focused on learning (as supported by the learning guide) and open to insights that could take you in unexpected directions.

Tools in This Section

This section introduces the final tools in the design thinking tool kit. **Customer co-creation** invites a few potential customers to collaborate with you—by playing with rough prototypes—in order to develop an offering that truly meets their needs. During the **learning launch**, you then take an improved prototype into the market for an extended experiment designed to test the remaining key assumptions that stand between your concept and its full commercial development. Now, instead of "trying this at home," we are ready to try it in the market.

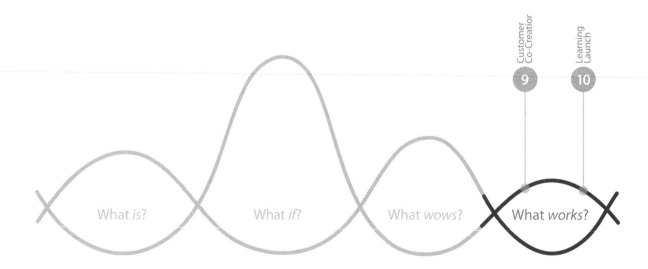

Customer Co-Creation

Learning Launch

9

10

What *is?*   What *if?*   What *wows?*   What *works?*

CHAPTER ELEVEN:
CUSTOMER CO-CREATION

Customer co-creation is the process of engaging a potential customer in the development of new business offerings. It involves putting some prototypes in front of potential customers, observing their reactions, and using the results to iterate your way to an improved offering. A typical co-creation phase might have three rounds, each embodying the changes and improvements that emerged from the preceding round.

If you want your innovations to be meaningful to your customers, to be worth investing in both financially and psychologically, you need to invite them into your process. This creates energy and passion, for managers as well as those they serve. If you want to be truly customer-centric, customer co-creation is not an option—it should be a requirement any time funds are allocated to a growth project.

When to use it: The sooner the better! In our Six Sigma world, which values perfection and polish, we tend to get anxious about showing customers unfinished, unpolished "stuff." Get over it. Innovation is about learning, and customers have the most to teach you. The sooner you get something in front of them that they can react to, the faster you'll get to a differentiated value-added solution. And they will love being involved.

Why customer co-creation de-risks your growth project: Customer co-creation is among the most value-enhancing, risk-reducing approaches to growth and innovation. Any time you introduce an unfamiliar concept, you can expect to get it mostly wrong. That is why co-creation, using low-cost, low-fidelity prototypes, is so essential to reducing the risks and improving the speed of successful innovation. Co-creation takes a week or two and costs four figures or less, whereas formal new-product rollouts require months and cost six figures or more. For this reason, we view co-creation as one of the most significant ways to de-risk a growth project.

If your organization appears dead set on placing a big bet, with all the attendant risks, don't think of co-creation as contrarian behavior. Instead, think of it as a parallel effort to guide how that bet gets placed. The output of co-creation is not limited to identifying problems; it also identifies potential solutions, which means the results can be embraced by the larger organization.

Getting Started

There is no rocket science to effective customer co-creation—just a few simple principles. These have to do with picking the right customers to invite to your playgroup, giving them something worth playing with, and listening attentively to their feedback. You may not have done this before, but, like Dave Jarrett, once you try it you will never go back to your old ways. Diane Ty also found some good uses for co-creation, and we will highlight her story as we share some tips to guide you along.

1. **Enroll customers who care about you** (but not as much as they care about themselves). You need customers you trust (they are being exposed to your possible future plans), who are hungry for a solution and motivated to be completely candid.

2. **Diversity = security.** Enroll a diverse group of customers for co-creation sessions. There is a temptation to choose only target customers, but you may be surprised to learn that non-target customers are just as keen for what you have to offer. In developing the cleaning system that became Swiffer, P&G worked with professional cleaning crews, stay-at-home moms, and residents of college fraternity houses (that team had courage!). All three groups contributed to the final version of Swiffer.

    Diane Ty and her AARP team organized two days of intensive co-creation sessions with target users. They used a meeting facility in Boston and recruited 20 individuals to participate in 90-minute individual sessions interacting with rough prototypes.

3. **Create a no-selling zone.** Co-creation sessions are not sales calls for your solution. A rule of thumb is that the customer should do 80 percent of the talking. As Dave Jarrett explains:

    > *"What the storyboard is really all about is not trying to sell you something; it's simply trying to understand if we were to approach something, how would you recommend we approach it? What would be valuable to you?"*

4. **Engage one customer at a time.** This may seem inefficient, but remember that you are not going for a statistically significant sample size. You will learn so much more when there is no social pressure on the research subjects— when they are alone with you and not influenced by others expressing their opinions at the same time.

5. **Offer a small menu of choices.** Presenting a single concept, well considered, defies the purpose of co-creation. Typically, you want to give customers two or three options and invite them to begin exploring one that they are drawn to. Maybe they can move on to a second one, if time allows. Simply learning that your favorite concept is not the one customers choose first can be important.

   Be sure to include choices you think people will *not* select. The best firms test concepts that they suspect are too extreme or too tame, just to locate their customers' novelty threshold. Sometimes customers will surprise you. The managers who oversaw the Google Gmail alpha test predicted it would come across as too intrusive (a software algorithm reads your private e-mail and serves you targeted ads?). But they tested it anyway, and Gmail became a smash success.

   > The AARP co-creation sessions were designed to help Diane and her team understand not only which of their concepts were appealing but also how the Gen Y audience wanted to interact with AARP's possible offerings. These were explained on paper cards, using illustrations and a descriptive sentence or two, such as:
   >
   > - AARP provides simple person-to-person loan templates
   > - Compare my budget to those of relevant peers
   > - Tool to visualize my life financial plan, with scenarios
   >
   > The card format was used so that individuals could bundle the cards together to create a complete AARP offering optimized to their needs. Each user sorted concept cards into categories of "critical," "important," and "nice-to-have."

6. **Provide visual stimulus, but leave it rough.** If you want people to walk with you into a possible future, you need to help them *see* it. But nothing fancy at this stage; quick sketches or posters are all you need. You want to keep the visual fidelity of your prototypes *low* in the early iterations to reinforce your willingness to modify

the solution on the basis of customers' input. Make your prototype too polished and they may feel that the right answer is, "Looks great!"

As Diane Ty of AARP explains it:

"The most critical thing is not being afraid to make a mistake. You have to be willing to make a call and then if you're wrong, be okay with that—this is a big leap of faith for me because I have a bit of a perfectionist mentality. To put stuff out there that's unfinished is hard. But I know that it's going to be a net positive because whatever my team and I put together will only get us a certain percentage of the way there. To make it really good I needed to be okay with getting it out there unfinished to then get the consumer input to make it better and closer to what it needed to be."

Leaving parts of the concept incomplete is a great way to elicit the customer's creativity and competence. Even if you know how your firm will want to fill in the blank spaces, it can be illuminating to see what actual users come up with. For example, AARP presented a rough paper prototype of its Life Plan Visualization concept to co-creation participants with the "Understand Your Nest Egg" tool. Listening to participants describe what they would expect to find after they clicked the button at the bottom, AARP team members realized that a Life Plan Visualization would most likely be used for self-education and self-motivation instead of for planning.

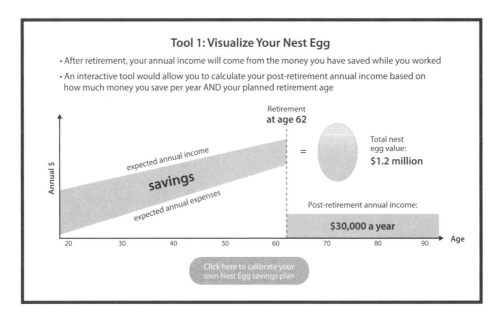

Tool 1: Visualize Your Nest Egg
- After retirement, your annual income will come from the money you have saved while you worked
- An interactive tool would allow you to calculate your post-retirement annual income based on how much money you save per year AND your planned retirement age

Example Invitation to a Co-Creation Session

Subject: Request for participation in product development

Hello,

I am writing to invite you to participate in a research session that my firm is conducting to aid product/service development. My firm, COMPANY NAME, is a TYPE OF COMPANY and we wish to gather insights about the needs of CUSTOMER/STAKEHOLDER GROUP and how several new product/service concepts could be improved. This is an exciting opportunity for you to contribute your expertise and ensure that the products/services we develop meet your needs.

Our primary research goal is to better understand the NEEDS/ROLES/TASKS OF STAKEHOLDER GROUP so that we can help find innovative ways to serve you better. We are currently recruiting participants for our research. You and/or members of your team are ideal participants because of your experience and expertise.

During the 90 MINUTE research interview and activity session, we will be asking you to share your experience and insights into NEEDS/ROLES/TASKS. We understand that your time is extremely valuable. We would like to offer a $200 donation to the charity of your choice, in thanks for participating in our research. We would also like to provide a letter of thanks documenting your contribution of expertise and thought leadership; past participants have requested these letters for their HR personnel files.

May I follow up with you via telephone to share more about this research study and discuss potential participants from your team?

Thank you. I look forward to speaking with you.

Best Regards,

YOUR NAME
YOUR CONTACT INFORMATION

7. **Help customers communicate visually.** Providing simple, visual ways for customers to express their choices helps them tap into their true preferences rather than tell you what they think you want to hear. Dave Jarrett's red and green stickers are a perfect example. Leaving empty speech bubbles over a character in a storyboard is another way to elicit opinions. The card-sorting approach used by AARP is yet another mechanism for communicating with customers.

8. **Leave time for discussion.** In co-creation, the discussion is more important than the actual choices customers make. Sometimes, we film their faces so we can note when they make a choice they don't really believe in. These areas of dissonance are also often revealed through clarifying questions. Answering questions with questions (within reason) is another good technique. If the customer asks, "How would private information be handled?" the best response is, "How would you recommend it be handled?"

    > As the AARP users examined and sorted the cards, they described how and when they would use each element. By the 20th interview in five days, the patterns were becoming clear to the AARP team. Several key themes emerged, including:
    >
    > - A clear need for a financial vocabulary for communication among people with shared finances (for instance, parents and their adult children)
    > - A distrust of any self-help tool that included sales offers
    > - A strong (and surprising) trust in institutional and expert authority (again, as long as nothing was being sold, and the trust was largely due to AARP's nonprofit status)

9. **Provide timely feedback.** Customers don't care if the prototype is low-fidelity or if the idea is embryonic and half-baked, but they do want to know you used their input to refine it. So let them know what you did with their input. That is part of the co-creation contract.

Despite its merits, co-creation is a term that may be unfamiliar and even off-putting to senior leaders. So call it "getting the voice of the customer." In a recent co-creation session, Siemens experimented with a simple storyboard as part of a new offering, using blank speech bubbles in key panels. Their prospective customers wrote comments in the bubbles to show where they were pleased, confused, or frustrated. When the team shared these findings back at the office, senior management pored over the customer feedback as if it were a revelation. These early comments directly shaped the offering that was launched several months later.

Small wins like this will earn you permission for broader explorations. You will be able to conduct co-creation in broad daylight. Senior leaders will begin to ask, "How did customers respond to the prototype?" In time, you will employ customer co-creation on every growth project as the best way to understand **What** *works*.

Try This at Home

Consider a process that is mostly within your control: how you conduct annual reviews with key subordinates. Let's try an experiment in which you enroll a key subordinate (we'll call her Ellen) to co-create her annual review process.

1. Find a blank whiteboard (or a flip chart) and create a five-panel storyboard. Draw as simply as you can.

   - Panel 1: Supervisor with thought bubble: "It's time for Ellen's annual review. She is really important to me and has a lot of potential. She deserves my best effort."
   - Panel 2: Ellen reading an e-mail with a thought bubble:
     - Version 1: "Let me make a summary of what I've worked on, and what I've accomplished, to assist my supervisor in collecting data."
     - Version 2: "My supervisor will give me a list of my key projects that will be under consideration."
     - Version 3: "I will submit a list of people who should provide input for my evaluation."
     - Version 4: Other (room for subordinate to fill-in)
   - Panel 3: Supervisor gathering data from key people
     - Version 1: Detailed data from three people
     - Version 2: High-level data from six people

- Panel 4: Reviewing the feedback

  – Version 1: A single meeting with written feedback and a discussion
  – Version 2: Written feedback first, then a meeting
  – Version 3: A pair of meetings, one for feedback and one for future planning

- Panel 5: Ellen reflecting on the review process five years in the future, with a thought bubble about what it signified for her: "Hmm, I remember that review. It really taught me _____."

2. Invite Ellen to discuss the storyboard with you. Ask her which alternatives she likes. What does she like about them? What is missing?

3. Follow the ground rules of co-creation: Observe and listen at first, to learn as much as possible without being too directive. Shift to more direct questions and discussion during the final ten minutes.

4. Reflect on what you learned. Did the storyboard help Ellen give you some new insights about the process? Do you understand the annual review process differently than you did before the co-creation session?

CHAPTER TWELVE

LEARNING LAUNCH

A **learning launch** is an experiment conducted in the marketplace quickly and inexpensively. It forms a bridge between customer co-creation and commercial rollout. In fact, think of the learning launch as customer co-creation in 4D, incorporating both the physical and the *time* dimension. In contrast to a full new-product rollout, a learning launch's success is about not how much you sell but how much you *learn*. The goal of the launch is to test the remaining critical assumptions about why this is an attractive business idea (which you surfaced during **What** *wows* and have already subjected to thought experiments, where appropriate). It is the next level of assumption testing, but instead of thought experiments, you are investing in live experiments with actual customers, using the learning guide to keep you on track.

When to use it: Use the learning launch when you are ready to ask customers to put some skin in the game. Merely asking what they think, however useful for *developing* a new concept, is a weak form of *testing* it. The true test of a concept includes customers demonstrating their enthusiasm through their *actual behavior*, ideally over an extended period of time. Do they value it? Do they use it the way they said they would? Ideally, their behavior includes a willingness to part with cold hard cash. You need the answers to those questions before you commit to building a new offering.

Why a learning launch de-risks your growth project: A hallmark of design thinking is its ability to bypass the culture of debate and help managers learn through action in the marketplace. As we've discussed before, using historical data to predict an offering's market performance has some severe limitations. After a point, we actually *increase* our risk by focusing on analysis instead of experimentation. Our investment—both financial and emotional—gets higher and higher, making it likely that we will fall in love with our new concept and screen out the data that tell us about our beloved's flaws. "Marry in haste, repent at leisure" applies to business, too. So you need to understand the reality of what your bets are based on. This requires taking the assumptions surfaced during assumption testing and figuring out what data you'll need to really test them—and where you'll get that data.

Learning launches come after co-creation and before pilots. Unlike a co-creation session, learning launches need to feel real to both launchers and customers. And unlike a pilot, a learning launch needs to be tightly constrained during execution but open to major changes at the end. Pilots are usually focused on refinement before commercial launch and rarely lead to wholesale changes or tabling the project. The managers who run learning launches don't like to think of themselves as conducting experiments—they want to start a successful new business! But there is a fine line between having the passion to shepherd a nascent business through the obstacles that organizations and partners throw in its path and ignoring important data about its weaknesses.

Professors at Stanford's Design School advise aspiring designers to "treat your prototypes like they are right and your assumptions like they are wrong." We like that advice. A learning launch tries to find the line between the two approaches—and walk it.

Getting Started

Designing the launch itself is straightforward. First, you need a working prototype. Time to move from 3D to 4D (which is just a 3D experience that persists over time). To illustrate the keys to a successful learning launch, we will pick up where we left off with Brivo Systems, the e-commerce software firm.

By late October 2000, Mark Stein and his Brivo colleagues had reached two important milestones with the Oscar the Smartbox concept: They had finished a software application to manage e-commerce deliveries, and they had a scalable design for a smart mailbox to receive deliveries. Here's what Mark told us:

"We knew we had to attract a big manufacturing partner, like a Maytag or a Whirlpool, to take over the device if we were to hit a sub-$300 product cost. At that point, I think the pre-production units of Oscar cost close to $1,000 to make. We set our sights on the 2000 holiday season as the perfect time to prove the system really worked. So we created a market trial called the Brivo 100."

The Brivo 100 was guided by Mark's learning goals. If he had used a formal learning guide, as we recommend, it might have looked something like this:

Example Learning Guide for Brivo Systems*

1. Strategic Intent

Enable the last mile of e-commerce through an Internet-based software that (a) coordinates residential delivery of e-commerce packages and (b) provides closed-loop information to all parties to the transaction.

2. Remaining Key Assumptions to Be Tested

For this business concept to be successful, the following key assumptions must be true:

1. **Clear consumer value:** Consumers will appreciate the convenience of an unattended delivery option and be willing to pay a recurring fee ($15 to $20).
2. **Acceptable aesthetics:** Consumers will find the aesthetics of a physical delivery device (the Oscar unit) acceptable at their homes.
3. **Acceptance by carriers:** All major carriers (USPS, FedEx, UPS) will be willing to deliver to an Oscar unit.
4. **Manufacturing partner:** A branded manufacturer will be willing to build, market, and distribute the Oscar units.
5. **Security and survivability:** The Oscar units are secure and can survive in cold weather.
6. **Sub-$300 unit cost:** The Oscar units can be manufactured at scale for a sub-$300 cost.

3. In-Market Test Plan

The untested assumptions to be explored during the learning launch include:

Untested Assumption	Success Metric for Learning Launch
1. Clear consumer value	Consumers make at least six transactions during the 40-day trial period
	Post-trial survey shows >90% prefer Oscar to trips to UPS, etc.
	Post-trial survey shows >50% likely to purchase

Untested Assumption	Success Metric for Learning Launch
2. Acceptable aesthetics	Post-trial survey shows >67% find aesthetics acceptable
3. Acceptance by carriers	>95% transaction success rate (note: "failure" includes carriers bypassing the Oscar when customers are home)
4. Security and survivability	<5% incidence of vandalism or weather failure

4. Financial Capital to be Expended

The Brivo learning launch will require the following capital resources:

- Nearly full-time focus of ten people for 7 weeks, at a weekly burn rate of $16,000 per week, for a total of $105,000

- Out-of-pocket expenses for rental trucks, customer incentives, etc., of $22,000

- Total financial capital to be expended = $127,000

*All statements, numbers, and timelines within this document are the supposition of the authors and do not reflect any learning guide used within Brivo Systems.

Mark Stein and his venture investors were clear that testing the critical assumptions would be worth the financial capital, even if the conclusions were discouraging and cast doubt on the viability of the business concept.

Your own learning guide should follow the same four-section format. The learning launch, then, is simply a market experiment that applies the resources in section four in the most efficient way to test the assumptions in section three. With a strong learning guide as your foundation, the project management skills you already have will get you most of the way to a successful learning launch, along with these success principles:

1. **Set tight boundaries.** Since this is a learning launch and not a pilot, it is important to plan for it to end. Set concrete limits on key variables, such as time, geography, number of customers, features, and partner firms. How long is long enough? Brivo set a clear goal: to deploy 100 preproduction Oscar units in the D.C. area for the month of December.

Brivo's boundaries were clear, and it conducted its learning launch in 40 days. This is fine for a start-up, but what about a large corporation? One protocol we like is to constrain a learning launch to 100 days. This best suits our human conditioning: We can be intensely focused for a fixed period (such as a school semester), and then we must look up, take a break, reflect on what we learned, and recharge for another push. McDonald's refers to these as 100-day bursts. If you are thinking that the only thing your organization is capable of doing in 100 days is forming a committee and creating a lot of PowerPoint slides, join the club. But you can't play the game that way and expect to win at the kind of innovation we are talking about. This is about placing small bets fast. Lem Lasher, head of the office of innovation at CSC, told us:

> "The most high-impact projects at CSC involve an ambitious goal, a high-level sponsor, modest budgets, and tight time frames. Those are the best conditions for solving something difficult."

However you choose to constrain the learning launch, you may need to put it in writing. (Formal agreements may also be necessary to address issues of confidentiality.) Whether the agreement is in writing or not, the customer expectations need to be crystal clear or you may have a "success disaster" on your hands, such as unhappy customers who don't understand why you are taking away their Oscar smartboxes.

2. **Design with a sharp focus on key assumptions.** Review the key assumptions that you identified and list the ones that have not yet been tested. From those, choose which ones can be tested through a learning launch. Mark Stein defined the Brivo 100 learning goals like this:

> "The device and the service were free, but we told users the expected retail price so we could get their feedback at the end of the trial. We gave them some Amazon.com gift certificates to get them started, maybe $50 worth. Our goals were something like six transactions per unit and a 95 percent success rate. A failure could be due to the device, the software, the delivery person not finding the Oscar unit, whatever."

Another key assumption he mentions—that they will need to reach a unit cost of less than $300 for the Oscar hardware—was *not* part of their learning launch scope. As you make your plans to test key assumptions, be sure to:

- See to it that the prototype reflects the key assumptions you need to test.

- Translate the assumptions you plan to test into **specific metrics**. Brivo set metrics for the number of transactions per unit and the success rate of transactions, for example.

- Be explicit about how you will **generate the data** you need, especially behavioral data. Brivo was able to see how often people logged into their Brivo account and took this as a signal of their interest in information about their online purchases.

- Be explicit about the search for **disconfirming data**. Buddhists have a saying: "When a pickpocket sees a saint, the only thing he sees are the saint's pockets." We need a more expansive view for a learning launch to succeed. Disconfirming data are observations that disprove your hypotheses. As we've said, they are the most valuable to find and the easiest to miss. While he didn't use the learning guide in the format we presented above, Mark Stein did keep a running list of "red flags" to pay attention to, which included each of the issues noted earlier. One in particular threatened Brivo's ability to provide closed-loop data for every shipping transaction: "Will carriers bypass the smartbox if the customer is at home?" That worry proved to be unwarranted. Data from the Brivo 100 proved conclusively that carriers always preferred the Oscar since it helped them complete their routes faster.

- Match the budget to an **affordable loss** calculation. Compare the learning launch budget to the key assumptions you will test: Is testing them worth the budget you can commit? If so, this meets the threshold of what we call *affordable loss*. That is, even if you walk away from the project after the learning launch, it was worth it to know if the assumptions were true. If it's not worth the cost, redesign the learning launch to become more affordable.

3. **Build a team that is both disciplined and adaptive.** Like the rest of the innovation activities we have talked about in this book, a learning launch is a team sport. And the composition of the team makes a difference. Yes, you want the passionate supporters of growth and innovation on the squad. But having a few skeptics around will ensure that you are not designing a test to give you the answers you want. Someone with a financial perspective is valuable—and project management skills are essential. As straightforward as it sounds, a learning launch can be devilishly difficult to grasp for managers schooled in traditional ways. Find someone who has done it before, and get that person on the team. Mark Stein commented on the cohesiveness of the Brivo team:

   "The Brivo 100 was probably my favorite time in the history of the company. Everybody was focused on a single goal. Usually there is a lot of divide and conquer, heads-down, even in a

start-up. And of course we had every problem you can imagine. I remember when we were get-
ting the units installed at customers' homes, we didn't have a very big field ops group, maybe
four people, so we created sign-up sheets for volunteers to go on an installation run. Everyone
in the company did at least one installation."

4.   **Work in fast feedback cycles.** The learning launch is when your growth project first makes contact with reality. Expect surprises and be prepared to respond quickly. For large enterprises, a weekly check-in meeting might be the right mechanism for feedback. At Brivo, the problems were many and the feedback loops were tight:

> *"For the first couple of weeks in December, we would hold daily check-in meetings at around*
> *9:30 at night. Basically the entire firm was there, and no one was complaining about their work*
> *hours. It was more like 'Hey, can I help?' There were real problems with setting the Oscar device*
> *so it could see the wireless network reliably—remember, this was 2000—and protecting Oscar's*
> *brain, which was a circuit board wired to a Blackberry radio, from getting wet. We fried quite*
> *a few brains during the first week until we came up with a modification that kept water away*
> *from the electronics. Then our field ops group had to go back out to every one of the Oscars and*
> *do brain surgery. We were all on the edge of our seats."*

Clearly, having a process for handling dissent, resolving conflicts constructively, and adapting on the fly is a great asset to a learning launch.

5.   **Make it feel real.** A successful learning launch must make it easy for all participants to suspend their disbelief. It needs to feel real to customers, partners, and your internal team. Everyone has something at stake. If it feels like a game or make-believe, then the behavioral data it generates are suspect. All that focus on keeping things from feeling too polished? Gone. The collateral materials should look like Apple launching a new i-gizmo. All that talk of testing multiple options? Gone. The learning launch asserts "Here are the features you need. Period." When the Brivo 100 went into action, the platform worked for all online vendors and all delivery agents: UPS, the U.S. Postal Service, and FedEx. Pricing should be real, too. If you need to give away the product or service at this point, as Brivo did, at least tell the customers what the price is and ask for their feedback.

6. **Have back-up plans for everything.** As Mark Stein noted, "We had every problem you can imagine." The question is, what do you do about them? He and his team created back-up Oscar "brains" (the electronics module) to replace the ones that fried because of water contamination. They trained overflow installation crews to manage the surge of installation demands. And they gave Amazon.com coupons to any customer who had a delivery problem.

The Importance of On-Ramps

The learning launch goes to great lengths to simulate how the solution will operate at scale, but often overlooked is how you will in fact get to scale. That is, how do customers learn about the offering, try it out, become users, and enlist others? We think of this as the on-ramp. Recently, Starbucks began giving morning coffee customers a coupon for $2 off any cold drink after 2PM. The coupon can be considered an on-ramp to a new Starbucks experience: the afternoon cold drink. The gutsiest on-ramp we've encountered is used by OnStar, which provides the hardware and the service for free for one year.

Remember the Siemens Reward Store to handle ad hoc customer requests? The success of that concept was predicated on a key assumption: that service technicians would voluntarily sign up for the rewards program. Only then could they actively provide ad hoc repair services for customers. So how did the company motivate service technicians to volunteer (that is, what was its on-ramp)? Siemens sent announcements about the new program to each technician's home address, on a post-card, with the rewards prominently displayed. That way, the spouse would see the program and ask, "Hey, are you enrolled in this? It looks great!" The result? More than 50 percent of the service technicians enrolled in the program during the first 100 days, and customer satisfaction levels returned to historical highs.

Learning launches should test your on-ramp strategy, if possible. If you leave it to marketing to figure that out later, you are putting the fate of your new growth project in their (overcommitted, underfunded) hands. If only we had a dollar for every manager we heard say, "The customers who use it, love it," we'd be rich. That means that too many potential customers never made it up the on-ramp to awareness, understanding, consideration, tryout, purchase, use, habitual use, and then advocacy. Those advocates are the ones who create tipping points for successful new services and products. Starbucks thinks so, and you should, too.

Social Technologies and Learning Launches

Learning launches have become easier in the past three years because they have gained a powerful new ally: social technologies. As growth teams begin to include more and more digital natives (workers under the age of 35), the field of play begins to reflect their tools of choice. Where once we had collaboration among teams of 12 or fewer, Google's prediction market software is enabling collaboration among twelve thousand, and Twitter is enabling conversations among a million or more people.

The backbone of social technologies are formed by Web 2.0, which Forrester Research defines in this way:

> *"Web 2.0 is a set of technologies and applications that enable efficient interaction among people, content, and data in support of collectively fostering new businesses, technology offerings, and social structures."*[1]

Note that we are not talking about the idea management systems that became popular a decade ago. Ideas are usually not the problem with innovation. When IBM saw Cisco begin to dominate the router market and Nuance emerge as the leader in speech recognition software, it didn't say, "Why didn't we think of that?" IBM had already thought of both those concepts (in fact, IBM developed them first). It just failed to act on them as growth opportunities.

The failure modes that keep IBM and others from capitalizing on their promising ideas include:

1. Failure to connect the concept to an unmet customer need
2. Failure to get it prioritized amid the sea of ideas and priorities
3. Failure to prototype or visualize it so others understand it
4. Failure to get live customers involved in shaping it

The social technologies that address these failure modes include **prediction markets** and **social networking** communities such as Communispace, LinkedIn, Twitter, Facebook, and blogs and wikis. Hallmark routinely explores new concepts within an online community, well upstream of formal in-market testing. In 2004, Kraft Foods used social technologies to foster a dialog about convenience foods and dieting. Consumers told Kraft they preferred to think about treats, not diet foods. This led to a discussion about portion-controlled treats or rewards, and the concept of 100 Calorie Packs was born. It turned into a blockbuster for Kraft, all on the basis of what was learned through social technologies.[2]

In the field of prediction markets, fast-growing firms such as Crowdcast and Inkling improve forecasts by generating crowd wisdom. However, their methods are proving equally adept at letting people engage with nascent concepts and shape them into robust new growth platforms.

Across the board, social technologies are fundamentally changing how we interact with colleagues and customers (not to mention friends and strangers). Consider how AARP used a proprietary social network to develop the Life Plan Visualization concept into the offering that was to become its award-winning LifeTuner community:

> Based on what Diane and her team learned during their card-sort co-creation sessions, AARP developed a functional web prototype of the napkin pitch for the Life Plan Visualization concept. But they were not finished with co-creation. The next thing they did was organize a private online community of 400 young adults with the social networking community Communispace:

> *"The online community was designed to really give us the ability to test and learn our way into it and iterate around the design of our prototypes. We basically created a 24/7 focus group with them, putting four to five activities or surveys, discussions, brainstorms in front of them every week for a little over a year, to the point where we felt that they were co-creators in our whole product development process. And we got to the point where we didn't want to do anything until we bounced it off them.*

> *We would give them a link to a prototype that was on our staging site for them to take a look at and get input on the design, the user interaction. We would take wire frames and screen shots at all different levels of completion and put those in front of the young people and basically say 'Click here, take a look at this, tell us what you think,' that kind of thing. We showed them the house as it was being built, at all different stages, to get their feedback.*

> *We were doing some probing around the AARP brand and one of the users just hijacked that discussion and said, 'What I really want from AARP is a way to connect with your members. They have experiences that could really help us, and I want to talk to people older than me who are not necessarily my parents.' Many of the other Communispace participants chimed*

in and said 'Great idea!' We were really surprised—they really wanted a way to connect with mentors. That led to a feature on the site called 'been there' and the sharing of these stories, 'been there, done that.' The idea is absolutely spot on and very unique to AARP."

Digital environments like Communispace offer great opportunities for virtual co-creation. In fact, the potential of social networking for co-creation and learning launches has only begun to be tapped. You can learn from target customers you may never even meet!

LEARNING LAUNCH FOR PFIZER'S PAVLOV

Think back to Chapter 2, where we told you about Pfizer Consumer Healthcare's efforts to reinvigorate the Nicorette brand by designing a broader smoking cessation service. Developed under the code name Pavlov, the service first made contact with actual customers during a learning launch in Norway in early 2006. Naturally, Lauri Kien Kotcher, a senior vice president of global marketing, and other Pfizer executives wanted to see how the delivery system worked, and they wanted to learn whether smokers would be more successful in their attempts to quit.

They also had learning goals for their channel strategy. Would Pavlov sell from pharmacy shelves, like Nicorette? Or would it be more successful sold through employers, which bear the health insurance cost for employees who smoke? The final option was online, a channel that was relatively unfamiliar to Pfizer at the time. During the Norway trials, Pfizer tested all three channels and discovered that the vast majority of sales occurred *online*. This was perhaps the single most valuable discovery of the learning launch.

Transitioning to Scale-Up

Ultimately, learning launches need to result in *decisions*. If you have tested key assumptions, you should also be able to make concrete decisions about if and how to move ahead with the growth project. If you decide not to move ahead, think "table" and not "kill." Chances are, if a concept is strong enough to get to the learning launch stage, its problems may be temporary. Times change and so do enabling technologies, customer readiness, and so forth.

If you decide to move ahead with additional development investments, the learning launch should inform which features to improve, which customer segments to focus on, and myriad other aspects of a typical new-product-development process. In fact, one outcome of a learning launch could be that the project moves into a traditional development phase. Which means that design thinking has done its job. By following the design thinking process, we have de-risked the project by:

- Exploring current reality and framing a challenge (**What *is***)
- Generating new possibilities for growth (**What *if***)
- Testing assumptions and refining and prototyping the concept (**What *wows***)
- Enrolling customers to shape it into something we can execute (**What *works***)

There was still real development work left for Brivo before it could commercialize its last-mile-of-e-commerce solution, but the nature of the risks changed significantly after the Brivo 100 learning launch. As Mark Stein told us:

> *"If I think about what we learned in that 40-day period—wow! It did a lot for the company. It helped us close a B-round [of venture financing] and get a manufacturing partnership. And it taught us a lot about our software, our team, and our customers and partners."*

Brivo was ready to shift from exploration mode (dealing with unknown unknowns) to problem-solving mode (dealing with known unknowns). Diane Ty's LifeTuner team was ready for a similar shift after its yearlong interactions within the Communispace customer community.

So this is what success in the **What *works*** stage looks like:

> Reducing the unknowns to a discrete list of challenges you are confident you can solve through existing processes within the firm.

Leading Growth and Innovation
in Your Organization

As we conclude our design journey with a look at how to apply what you've learned in your organization, we want to introduce you to one more manager turned design thinker. Jacqui Jordan, although she hails from Down Under, sounds a lot like the other managers we've met. Schooled in a traditional business approach, Jacqui had headed the strategy group in the Business Banking unit of Suncorp, one of Australia's largest insurers, for ten years when she discovered design. There was no turning back:

> *"Real people in real organizations can actually do this! And once you understand the concept, you feel totally compelled to act on it. Your current way of working becomes intolerable, and design seems like the solution to so many problems. However, it's only when you are brave enough to start that you realize your brilliant solution comes with a whole swag of problems all of its own. The biggest challenge in my own design journey was acknowledging that it's okay that I haven't been to design school, and even though I don't work for IDEO or Google I can make design work for me in my world. It is possible to bring the power of design and imagination to the most traditional organizations—even an insurance company."*

Jacqui is now in charge of rolling out the approach across the business and has demonstrated design's ability to add value to tasks as diverse as increasing market share in the broker distribution channel, improving the claims experience, and even integrating two very different corporate cultures. In 2007, when Suncorp merged with Promina, another large Australian insurer, the design project that helped support the merger integration drew attention throughout the organization for its results. Jacqui's boss, Mark Milliner, described some of them:

> *"The Australian market for commercial insurance was shrinking at 8 percent per year. We got 1 percent growth in Year 1 and 8 percent in Year 2, post merger. We're getting 9 scores on customer satisfaction, versus 6 or 7 before. Insurance profits are very strong. We've got good staff engagement—at 80 percent, it's far better than the Towers Perrin Financial Services average, and I've got people who are passionate about the business. We've built something new together that people really believe can go to interesting places."*

But Jacqui had seen other design approaches that didn't have such happy endings:

> *"I've watched teams work hard to implement a textbook- theory-based approach. The ideas were great but seemed so different from our normal way of working that they couldn't get confidence from the business to try their approach. The team was looking to make a big impact, they were looking for big problems and permission to implement design methodology from end to end. In effect, they took an 'all or nothing' approach (because that's what the theory prescribed) and, not surprisingly, 'nothing' won."*

Starting small and keeping a low profile, Jacqui found, was the best way to introduce design to a traditional corporate setting:

> *"It's okay to start small. Rather than full immersion, I found it easier and less overwhelming to select a couple of design tools to implement in each project. Over the last couple of years, we've continued to build our design tool kit, but we still don't reference it openly as a design methodology. I think this has helped us avoid resistance and just focus on the work itself and let our outcomes do the talking for us. I don't think you need to be overt about calling design thinking 'design thinking.' In my world this just freaks people out and makes them nervous. One of the best things we did was keep relatively quiet about our application of design tools: we just gradually integrated them into our existing strategy processes and continued to refine and embed what worked."*

Focusing on business outcomes was also essential, she believed:

> *"You know that expression about common sense not being that common? That's why linking design to growth is so obvious yet so necessary. I think people really need to call this out specifically and back it up with some good practical examples, and demonstrate the relationship between design methodology and tangible business outcomes. I think this issue is one of the main reasons that design struggles in big corporations: It's viewed as being pro-customer, pro-staff, but not pro-profit!"*

Different Methods, Different Outcomes?

In the preceding pages, you have met a handful of design thinkers and design project teams, and you have taken a look at their methods. As we noted in Chapter 1, design thinking isn't a *substitute* for analytic thinking. It is a distinctly different way of approaching a growth problem—a different way of *knowing*. But does it produce a better outcome?

Jacqui Jordan at Suncorp is a believer in design thinking for more than just philosophical reasons. She started small and built momentum by integrating design thinking into existing processes and by delivering results the organization believes in—such as revenue growth in a shrinking market and significant share gains in a broker channel with cutthroat competition.

What about the other design thinkers we met?

Diane Ty and her team at AARP are basking in the glow of that most rare event—a great new idea that worked! The LifeTuner site launched on October 27, 2009. Within the first month, traffic to the site exceeded the goals set for month seven. In less than six weeks, the site had attained a Google rank of 5 because of the quality of its links. The new brand scores in the 97 percent range according to social influence measures, and the participation of the expert community tripled in the first six months, with users' questions answered in less than 24 hours, often by more than one expert. In June 2010, LifeTuner won the gold medal in the most prestigious global design competition, the IDEA awards. The entry noted that the project did exactly what strategy projects are supposed to do: produce important insights and use them to generate value for both customers and the sponsoring organization. But to those who understand life in large mature organizations, the story is much bigger than that. As *BusinessWeek* noted: "More than just a surprising offering from a well-known organization, LifeTuner shows that innovation is even possible within a cautious, tradition-bound group that itself is more than a half-century old."[1]

The design thinking team at Pfizer Consumer Healthcare also created a win. The Pavlov project for smoking cessation was launched in 2007 as ActiveStop and has become a market success in more than a dozen countries. It has restored growth and luster to Nicorette while helping many more smokers become ex-smokers. More detailed data are not available because Pfizer Consumer Healthcare was bought in 2008 by Johnson & Johnson. Part of the economic value created by the Pavlov team is represented in the acquisition price.

Kaiser Permanente's **Christi Zuber** began her design thinking journey in 2003. She and her colleagues in Kaiser's innovation consultancy have applied design thinking to a wide range of health care challenges, including medication dispensing, nursing shift changes, and ambulatory clinic design. In seven years, they have developed confidence and gained momentum from a string of successes born of user-centered design, rapid prototypes, and a tolerance for fast failures.

Dave Jarrett, the partner at Crowe Horwath, lives in the ultimate show-me culture: public accounting. But he, too, found enough proof in the design thinking approach to tell us that his firm had "saved ourselves a fortune," all because they stopped building sophisticated prototypes that customers did not want.

Our other accountant/consultant, **Mark Stein**, did not fare as well with Oscar, the smart mailbox. After a successful learning launch, Brivo landed a manufacturing partnership with Maytag. But after a management shake-up there, no one was left to carry forward a deal with a tiny start-up. Without a brand-name manufacturer that had nationwide distribution, the Brivo business model—speculative to begin with—was toast.

Surrounded by Oscar prototypes and shelves of spare Oscar "brains," Mark and then-CTO Steve Van Till discovered a surprisingly ripe alternative market: access control for commercial buildings. The software was perfect for using the Internet to open building doors. In effect, Brivo eliminated the need for a large manufacturer by substituting existing *buildings* for the smart mailbox.

Ten years later, the Brivo Access Control System is a market-leading solution for letting employees in and out of commercial buildings. Recently, however, the memory of Oscar was revived. Steve, now Brivo's CEO, told us:

> *"It's funny, but our system is being used today by a major retailer for what they call 'dark delivery'*
> *(aka, unattended delivery). This would make the final production evolution of Oscar, but with*
> *a large building as the box and a loading dock instead of a door."*

So, despite what appeared to be a successful learning launch in December 2000, Oscar never made it into commercial production. But was it a failure? We say absolutely not because the only failed design project is one that doesn't test the crucial hypotheses.

The most common reason that managers don't get to test their hypotheses is that they never even get a chance to conduct the experiment. And the reasons for that usually have more to do with what is happening *inside* their organizations than outside it. We know that the greatest barriers to growth and innovation in most organizations are not about competitors and customers and market conditions; they are about the organization's internal army of designated doubters exercising their veto power before you even have the chance to try.

Introducing a design thinking approach is not easy. Think back to Chapter 1 and the stark contrast we drew between the assumptions, mind-sets, values, and practices behind the traditional MBA's approach and those behind the designer's approach. Even the widespread recognition of the need for new approaches doesn't guarantee a smooth path. As Jacqui explained:

> "As the layers and dynamics of our operating environments become more complex and evolve more rapidly, it's no surprise that traditional linear problem-solving methodologies are either too slow or just don't work. But people fail to realize that the solutions to these big uncomfortable complex problems don't seem that comfortable either. I think there's something about people associating even the idea of a solution as offering reassurance. As managers we are often solutions looking for a cause—we are so quick with answers. Design unsettles people because we don't pretend to know the answer, and so much of our interest is with the problem, rather than its solution."

Five Tips for Getting It Right on Your First Try

Each of the design thinkers we've met in this book had a first time—an instance when, bolstered by their confidence in the power of design thinking, they ventured to apply it inside their own organizations. In this book, we've focused mostly on the process they followed, but now we must tell you that it wasn't always easy for them to set out on the design thinking path, especially for those who were in large, established organizations. The good news is that our design thinkers passed along a lot of practical advice for how to make your design thinking debut a smashing success:

1. **Pick your challenge ("to design think or not to design think").** Remember when you first learned how to whistle, and that was all you wanted to do? It drove everyone crazy. Design thinking can be like that. You can find a use for it anywhere, but it may not be the optimal tool for, say, running an operations meeting. Design thinking isn't a paradigm shift, rendering all other forms of problem solving obsolete. It is merely a different problem-solving approach, optimized for certain classes of problems. To decide whether you have a good opportunity for design thinking, ask yourself whether the problem or challenge you are facing is about:

- exploring unknown possibilities (rather than exploiting known certainties)
- creating elements of value and differentiation that do not exist yet
- unlocking new growth opportunities in an unfamiliar context
- tackling complex problems that have resisted other methods

Another aspect of picking the right challenge is paying attention to who else cares about it, especially if you are tackling something big (we'd rather you didn't, but more on that in a moment). "You need strong executive sponsorship before you take on a big design project," Jacqui Jordan told us. "There were a couple of times when the only thing holding everything together was Mark's endorsement. I can't tell you how critical this was to this project."

Our earlier research on successful growth leaders in mature organizations supports Jacqui's viewpoint.[2] When we queried managers about the extent to which the organization's systems and processes supported their growth initiatives, a whopping 50 percent told us their organizations actively inhibited their ability to grow their business, but more than 80 percent told us that they had supportive executive sponsorship. That suggests to us that you can end-run your firm's systems and processes and succeed—but you can't end-run your boss!

There are many positive sides to executive sponsor interest. The contributions you expect from senior managers include:

- Resources: time, people, expense budget
- Cloud cover to shield you from organizational barriers
- Access to influential colleagues
- Access to external resources
- Permission to access customers and partners
- Dynamic decision-making support for when the project needs to shift direction
- Purpose: the sense that this project matters a great deal

Obviously, if you hold out for a boss who already loves design thinking, you could wait a *long* time. To get started, you need a boss with an open mind, who *gets* what you are trying to do and understands the logic (but not necessarily the tools and practices) behind a design approach. You never know where you will find such a person, but rest assured that they are not just in marketing. Our stereotypes are often wrong. At Suncorp, a group in accounting turned out to be enthusiastic design thinkers (after protesting that they couldn't possibly do that kind of thing); Christi Zuber discovered the same thing with her clinicians, and so did Dave Jarrett with his bankers and tax experts.

Finally, it is important to pick a problem that has some urgency behind it. And then frame your goals in language and metrics (lowering costs, increasing revenues, improving customer satisfaction) that make sense to the people who really care about solving the problem.

If the challenge you face is worthwhile and lends itself to a design thinking approach, and you have a supportive sponsor, you are ready. The next step is to scope the design thinking effort: How big is it, and what resources will you need to get it done?

2. **Think small.** Resist the urge to supersize your early design efforts. This advice was echoed by just about every manager who had succeeded with design thinking. As Jacqui points out, a lot of the trouble managers get themselves into when they pursue organic growth is due to the misguided advice to "think big." For every spectacular success, there are many painful failures. Yes—eventually you will need to ensure that the growth opportunities you identify are sufficiently scalable to interest your organization. But the time to do that is later, after you've had one or two (or maybe even more) spins through the hypothesis testing process and have eliminated as much uncertainty as possible, especially around the value creation test.

Christi Zuber, at Kaiser, offered similar advice:

> "If you start out with this big bang thing so everybody in the organization is looking and you've got everything on the line—that's not a great place to start. Automatically you're dealing with such a pressure-cooker situation that you're not setting yourself up to succeed. It's like learning how to ride a bike. You're not going to start at the top of the mountain and do downhill mountain biking the first time you ever jump on a bike. You're going to start with training wheels in a driveway. We need to start small and to learn our way into a new skill set, because it is a different way of thinking. We didn't have the expectation that the first time we did this that we were going to solve world hunger. We all knew that we were trying to find a way of creating solutions that were meaningful for our organization. We knew we had to have patience with each other

as we learned along the way. So, go easy on yourself! Realize you've got to start off with training wheels, but that's okay—that's the way that we learn.

Build your design thinking muscles by tackling some small challenges first: fixing the employee orientation process, for example, or introducing a weekly customer report. These are just-do-it-size projects that don't require permission, a big announcement, an ongoing team, or an expense budget—and therefore they don't set off the risk management process. You may have done several of these already, but try one or two more using the tools from this book that are new to you.

3. **Select and manage your team carefully.** The merits of multidisciplinary teams have been drilled into managers for over two decades, yet we still confuse "diverse" with "politically inclusive." For design thinking projects, it's true diversity you're after. Think of your team's design potential as bounded by the experience base of everybody on it. This is your collective wisdom. If you all look alike, you don't have much to work with. Different parts of the project require different skills, strengths, and experience: Involving multiple departments, while important, is not enough. You need hypothesis generators and hypothesis testers—or what one manager we know called "starters" and "finishers." The best-performing teams have these attributes:

- A strong-willed, passionate leader who remains confident in the process despite the uncertainty of the result (a tricky but essential balancing act)

- Diversity of skills, including:

    – Observation and listening

    – Framing and strategy

    – Analysis

    – Visualization and storytelling

    – Organization and management

    – Low ego needs—collective wisdom will lie dormant if a dominant personality squelches debate

    – Co-location and a flexible, collaborative physical space

    – A shared purpose

    – A formal extended team

THE WAR ROOM

Envision a physical space where you put stuff all over the walls. All the photos you gathered during the exploration phase, your experience maps and personas and descriptions, and maybe even your chili chart. It's a place where the growth project team can gather to share insights and feedback; it's a place that gives the team a cohesive identity, enables cross-functional collaboration, and greatly streamlines status reporting.

This is what we call a war room, and it's one of the best ways to maintain momentum on a design thinking project. At Microsoft, the Xbox development team established a war room in an undesirable space that had been set aside for visiting consultants (ouch!). Jon Hayes, the creative lead for Xbox, calls the war room a "fossil record" of the project. Any time an executive asked, "How is it going?" Jon said, "Come to the war room because we can't pack all this stuff up into PowerPoint." They literally could trace the decisions around the four walls and remember how they had gotten there. Every time you walked in, the room told the story of the project.

A complex project needs a formal **extended team** of functional experts to contribute at key points, but not consistently. Lining them up at the outset, even before their skills are required, can go a long way toward fostering speed and efficiency, a crucial factor for success.

Having a team is a great asset and a great responsibility. Designers bring a tremendous level of discipline to project management. Their image as artists belies an incredible attention to process and detail. To benefit from the diverse skills of the team, you will need to orchestrate individual work and group work, with frequent communication to coordinate the transitions. We recommend three team communication constructs, in addition to the project management aids, for successful collaboration. They are sometimes called "the three Ws":

- The **watering hole**: A shared physical space where people can meet and collaborate easily. If it has coffee and snacks nearby, so much the better. If it is in the form of a dedicated war room or project room, that is the best solution of all.

- The **work-in-process wall**: A section of wall large enough for work to be posted. It should be stocked with Post-its and markers so random comments can be made on a "drive-by" basis.

- The **weekly check-in**: A 60-minute weekly meeting that occurs at the same time every week and includes off-site contributors (by phone or video cam). Seeing is believing. These are working sessions to surface stress points and foster collaboration, and the materials should be functional, not showy. Our weekly check-ins always follow the same agenda, so there is no fussy preparation and people get accustomed to their roles.

As the project moves from **What *is*** to **What *if***, **What *wows***, and **What *works***, the demands on the team members vary widely. The three Ws provide a sense of order and continuity that can be a calming influence during the transitions.

External communications will be less frequent but are equally crucial. Most projects will have formal check-ins that align with the four questions of the design thinking process. This is where the project management aids come in handy (we suggest a careful review of the descriptions and templates in the Appendix). In addition, it is typical for higher-profile projects to attract ad hoc demands for external communications. If the project sponsor is positive and enthusiastic, these take the form of "information briefings" for various functional groups. If the sponsor is more a nervous Nellie, you and your team may be called on often to answer such questions as "How big is the market?" "Are you sure it will come in under budget?" and "What's the status update?" Executive sponsors of either stripe will benefit from a project that operates with high transparency. They may even appreciate a standing invitation to the weekly check-in meeting. If they attend, stick

EXAMPLE WEEKLY CHECK-IN AGENDA

The weekly check-in is purely a functional meeting. It happens every week at the same time, so preparation is a snap. We recommend a simple, repeatable format like this:

1. Roll call

    a. If someone is absent, who will get the results of this meeting to him or her?

2. Snapshot of where we are (usually a GANTT chart and a calendar)

3. Key activities, next five business days

    a. Items on the critical path
    b. Decisions to be made

4. Key activities, remainder of the project

    a. Items of greatest risk
    b. Advice / keys to success for managing them

5. Action items from this meeting

    a. Decisions made / changes to plan
    b. Action items
    c. Issues to be handled off-line

TEN TIPS FOR INNOVATING WITH SPEED

We noticed something curious in our research into the most successful growth leaders. They never mentioned speed as a key aspect of their work, yet we saw it in everything they did. Indeed, speed seems to be wired into growth leaders. To better understand how speed fosters success on growth projects, we convened a working group of 12 companies, including McDonald's and Kaiser Permanente, which shared their respective "cheat sheets" for speed. We then supplemented their tips with some we've gleaned from our own research:

1. Choose a burning platform as a place to start
2. Tell a human-centered story to arouse passions
3. Care about speed; make the words "by when?" part of every conversation
4. Agree on audacious goals
5. Agree on a fast decision-making model (who decides, when do they decide, using what criteria?)
6. Set public deadlines (but not too public!)
7. Don't debate; experiment (learn by doing)
8. Share your ideas when they are just "good enough" (have the courage to look foolish)
9. Let others validate your ideas
10. Speak the truth about failures (and what was learned)

to your agenda. Don't be tempted to turn a meeting into a dog-and-pony presentation.

4. **Manage your momentum.** In our experience, momentum is an underappreciated resource on an innovation project. As long as a project is clicking along and people feel productive, there is a positive buzz. The number one momentum builder is speed. Team members may complain about the fast pace, but those complaints are a soft pitter-patter compared with the deafening roar you hear when things slow to a crawl. The top three reasons things slow to a crawl? Slow decision making, slow decision making, and slow decision making.

Speed doesn't happen by itself. But forming a committee does not create momentum. Neither does having a meeting—even a good one. Momentum is fueled by the *energy* produced when groups of people work together to identify, create, and test great new value-enhancing ideas—and then see the fruits of their labor. Momentum runs on an emotional high, and like other highs, it doesn't last long. It dissipates as people go back to their real jobs. As an innovation leader, you've got to use that energy fast or lose it. The buzz coming out of the greatest brainstorming session ever doesn't survive a month's silence afterward.

Speed thrills. We don't fully understand why, but all the data we've seen about successful growth teams confirm that fact. A 2008 study by innovation strategy consultancy Peer Insight of the outcomes of 42 high-risk innovation projects (that is, NOT line extensions) in 26 global 500 firms revealed a striking correlation between speed of project execution and market outcomes. Projects that achieved "excellent" outcomes in the market (per the goals set by the firms themselves) took an average of 11.8 months to develop. Projects that achieved "good" outcomes required 16.6 months. And growth projects that were judged as "mediocre, poor, or failed" required 20.8 months.

But the kind of speed we are talking about is not simply overall time to market. Rushing ill-conceived solutions into the marketplace before you fully understand the customer's problem is the *opposite* of what design thinking is all about. What we are talking about here is the speed of learning, and shortening the cycle time as you iterate through progressive levels of hypothesis generating and testing.

There is an interesting tension between fast and slow in the design thinking process. Designers take the time to study a problem up front: Their solutions tend to fall naturally out of this immersion in **What *is***. As managers, we are often reluctant to take that kind of time at the outset for thoughtful reflection. We are in a hurry to get to solutions. Sadly, these top-of-mind solutions are rarely the kind that produce true innovation and growth. In our haste to find quick answers, we find inadequate ones that never identify the real value creation opportunity at all—and that's not really very efficient, is it?

Many senior executives act as though momentum is created by the risk management gates they erect. "I'll set a review meeting and hold them accountable for results!" is how the thinking goes. But that process isn't meaningful to the growth project team, which helps create the PowerPoint deck but often doesn't get transparency into the deliberations and funding decisions that ensue.

The inward focus of formal project reviews overlooks the most reliable source of momentum: the customer. Team members on AARP's LifeTuner cannot recall most of the project's internal management reviews, but they will never forget the customer co-creation sessions or customers' reactions to their initial concept tests. Putting concepts into the world—even a narrowly defined world such as an online customer panel—is pure adrenaline to a growth team. We believe wholeheartedly in management team reviews, as long as they focus on the right questions, such as, "How did the customer panel respond to the concept?" Put the internal reviews wherever you want; the real momentum of the project can be pegged to milestones where customers interact directly with the new concept as the project team observes.

5. **Be ready for moments of stark terror.** Talk about design thinking often sounds rosy and aspirational—a clear signal to the experienced manager to run, not walk, to the nearest exit. Jacqui warned us: "When I catch up with people who are genuinely trying to implement design, our conversations aren't about bragging about what we've accomplished; it's more like a therapy support group where we use reassurance and encouragement from others just to keep going."

In fact, there are predictable moments of truth in a design thinking project, moments that may precipitate feelings of stark terror and test your reserves of personal courage. It is said that forewarned is forearmed. In that spirit, we asked a group of respected design thinkers to share some of their moments of stark terror. Here are the top six, in chronological order.

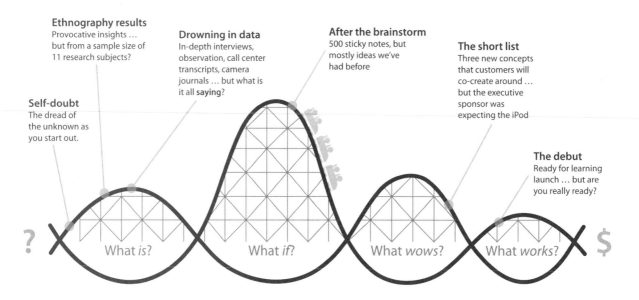

Ethnography results
Provocative insights … but from a sample size of 11 research subjects?

Drowning in data
In-depth interviews, observation, call center transcripts, camera journals … but what is it all **saying**?

After the brainstorm
500 sticky notes, but mostly ideas we've had before

The short list
Three new concepts that customers will co-create around … but the executive sponsor was expecting the iPod

Self-doubt
The dread of the unknown as you start out.

The debut
Ready for learning launch … but are you really ready?

?   What *is*?   What *if*?   What *wows*?   What *works*? $

The self-doubt moment. This is when it dawns on you: "I just promised *WHAT*? By *WHEN*? With only *WHAT* resources to get it done?" After pitching and re-pitching your project, you expected to enjoy the thrill of victory and instead are suffering the dread of the unknown.

What to do: Breathe. It feels this way only for a moment or two, like the pause before a roller coaster plunges downward. This is the feeling Joe Montana had before he led the touchdown drive that won the Super Bowl. Within minutes you will be in the arena, executing the plan, learning at a breathtaking pace, and (we predict) loving it.

The ethnography results moment. You are fresh from reviewing customer journey maps and other ethnographic research results, and you have a crystal clear sense of the latent need you can address. The executive sponsor then sees the sample of 11 customers, none of which appears similar to any others, and she says, "Are we going to make decisions based on *that*?"

What to do: Have compassion for the executive sponsor. She has had maybe 45 minutes to grasp the role of ethnographic research in the innovation process, whereas you have had at least 45 *hours* and possibly 45 *days*. Remind her that you are not looking for quantitative proof. Rather, this process is designed to help create hypotheses your competitors don't have. Your research is about *inspiring* new ideas, not proving them. That will come later.

The drowning in data moment. Your intense observation and interviewing of customers, plus all your secondary research, has produced mountains of data—so much that you have no idea how to begin making sense of it all.

What to do: Just start sorting. First, make big piles on top of your desk, batching the stuff in ways that make sense to you. Second, find a big blank wall and start putting the stuff up on it. You're creating your yard sale. Have faith; patterns will emerge.

The morning after (the brainstorm) moment. A typical brainstorming process generates at least 100 ideas and sometimes more than 500. When participants reflect on the results, they are likely to think (or say), "Interesting, but I don't think we discovered our next $500 million line of business." They may also think, "We've had 80 percent of these ideas before, and the other 20 percent are pie-in-the-sky."

What to do: Warn participants in advance that they may feel this way. That will give you credibility when you say, "These are not future lines of business; they are raw materials for forging innovative combinations that have not been tried before. Forming these is the next step in the process, and we will share the results with you. It doesn't matter what ideas we have had before:

Innovation is usually not about producing ideas nobody has ever thought of before; it's about creating better value for customers—and profit for ourselves—by combining elements into innovative business designs. Stay tuned and expect to be surprised."

The short list moment. This occurs when you have created three innovative combinations of elements, shaping them into offerings that you are ready to share with customers in co-creation sessions. You show the concepts to the executive sponsor, and he says, flatly, "What else have you got?" As if, by reviewing the 15 or 20 concepts that didn't make the cut, he could find something better.

What to do: Remind yourself of the disparity in your perspectives. Your sponsor has inside-out instincts based on years in the industry that do not match the outside-in insights from the design thinking process. Your job is to gently remind him that these concepts are prioritized on the basis of how well they address unmet customer needs (based on the design criteria he agreed to four weeks ago!). You say, "Solving for underlying customer needs has to be the first priority, remember? Let's take these into co-creation sessions and see how customers respond."

The debut moment. This occurs right before the project goes live for the first time, usually during the learning launch. Sometimes it is the executive sponsor who wants to abort immediately before take-off, and sometimes it is the team that says, "We are NOT ready."

What to do: Go back to your learning guide (the final project management aid) to remind yourselves how the learning launch reduces risk. You have an affordable execution plan, a willing customer, and a set of learning goals. Don't let perfection stand in the way of progress!

Making the Sale and Managing Up

Now for what may be the biggest challenge of all: *Selling design thinking in your organization.* For those contemplating a new role as apostles of design thinking, ready to go forth and convert the unwashed masses, we've got one word for you: STOP!

You've drunk the Kool-Aid; they haven't. Abstract debates about the definition of design thinking and how it differs from traditional analytic approaches won't add a cent to your bottom line—or engage your audience. So start *doing* design thinking and let the outcomes speak for themselves. At the outset, call it a tool for increasing customer satisfaction, or producing innovation, or identifying new growth opportunities (obviously our favorite). Describe it as a different approach to problem solving or a new way to think strategically. By all means, talk about business impact and results. Choose words that will resonate not only with senior executives but also with those whose problems you aim to tackle.

Even Claudia Kotchka, who was behind design thinking's highly successful introduction at Procter & Gamble, didn't call it design thinking early on or waste time arguing about why to do it:

> *"It was a long time before we started calling anything design thinking at P&G. We'd just say, 'Here's a different way to innovate, to solve problems.' We would take ten people from a business unit, all disciplines, and put them on a wicked problem. We never told them they were using design thinking methodology—ever. It wasn't important for them to know what it was called. All they had to know were the basic steps and how to approach the problem with a different mind-set."*

Many newcomers to design thinking feel the urge to immerse themselves in a new vocabulary, quit their day jobs, and become evangelists. By all means, embrace your newfound passion, but talk about it in plain language. The most effective ways of managing up have everything to do with how you communicate:

1. Tell human-centered **stories**
2. Supplement the stories with **data**
3. Provide **transparency** to the process
4. Share learning and (if possible) business **results**

Let's start with storytelling. Telling human-centered stories accelerates your ability to sell design thinking by making your ideas feel real to sponsors, customers, partners, and funders. It reduces the chances of the heartbreak we talked about earlier: not failing because you were never allowed to try.

How many times has Dave Jarrett told the story of the cartoon prototype of cars in a sales lot? How many times did the Brivo team refer to the picture of the charred package on the grill? How many times has Christi Zuber shown the images of nurses wearing prototype sashes for their medication dispensing rounds? These stories and images make abstract ideas tangible and relevant. They build comfort with these new methods. Just take care not to separate stories from data; they need each other. Audiences don't check their analytic appetites at the door just because you are good at weaving a yarn. Dave Jarrett generally punctuates his story of the cartoon prototype by contrasting it with the $25,000 software prototype that would typically have been built—and then discarded—in its place.

Once you get the design thinking project rolling, transparency will be crucial in your attempts to manage up. Nothing fosters trust in an unfamiliar process like direct sunlight. Our "Ten Tips for Innovating with Speed," on page 190, reflect many of the tenets of transparency. Don't slow down for senior leaders, but make everything visible and invite them to drop in without notice. Confident leaders will take you up on it out of keen interest; nervous leaders will show up out of fear. Let them see the raw concepts, the verbatim customer quotes, everything. There will still be moments of stark terror, but you will be prepared for them.

The final key to managing up is to share your results. This element is best managed with the fourth project management aid, the learning guide. It is easy to share the results if the project succeeds. Imagine how good it felt to Diane Ty's team at AARP when LifeTuner was announced as a winner of a 2010 IDEA award. By contrast, how do you think Mark Stein felt when he called his board members to say that Maytag was out as a manufacturing partner and that Oscar was probably dead?

If the commercial outcome falls short, so be it, as long as the learning goals were met. Brivo's venture investors had a strategic focus on home commerce, and the Oscar experience offered valuable lessons about that market space. All growth projects—the failed ones as well as the smashing successes—must answer a strategic question, and the design thinker's job includes communicating the strategic value of the knowledge capital that was gained.

Jacqueline LeSage Krause, head of the corporate innovation unit at The Hartford, is a firm believer in sharing the results of a project transparently, regardless of the outcome:

> *"Our charter includes being the 'white space' exploration group, so we know many of the projects we take on will 'fail' in conventional terms while still in our pipeline. And whatever the market outcome is, we have to harvest what was learned and provide that insight to the [business units]. I tell our team, 'We are the rapid learning unit. The only way to fail is if we fail to learn.' So we focus on figuring out 'What can we get out there quickly?' and 'What are the key things we need to learn in this next stage?' Return on knowledge is one of our key performance measures as a unit."*

Design Thinking Begins with Design Doing

When we set out to write this book, several expert designers advised us not to. "There is no such thing as design thinking, just design doing," one said. Another suggested that the best we could hope for was to help managers *appreciate* good design. Those views remind us of the Apple design "hairball" we showed you in Chapter 1. We hope that we have demonstrated—through the stories of managers without design training such as Dave Jarrett, Christi Zuber, and others—that the process of design can be untangled, made transparent, and harnessed by managers of many different backgrounds.

There is, however, a kernel of truth in the emphasis on *doing*. Design as a problem-solving tool is a contact sport. To see if design thinking can work for you, you must try it. That's why we've urged you throughout to *try this at home*. And that's why we invite you now to choose a growth opportunity (a small one), find a collaborator, and immerse yourself in **What** *is*. From that moment on, you are in the arena. A world of rapid learning will unfold before you, and **What** *if*, **What** *wows*, and **What** *works* are just around the corner. We promise, your growth projects will never be the same.

APPENDIX

THE PROJECT MANAGEMENT AIDS

Although design's *environment* is full of uncertainty, the *management* of your design project shouldn't be. The project management aids (PMAs) will help you get as much clarity, control, and transparency into the management of a design thinking project as possible. You also will find them to be invaluable for keeping senior executives informed.

The first PMA, the **design brief**, is most helpful at the beginning of the **What *is*** stage. As you set out to explore current reality, this PMA forces you to clarify your ambitions and constraints. It asks you to frame your design challenge, define its scope, and pose the key questions to explore at the outset: What do you expect to get out of this work? What would success look like? How will you know if the project added value?

Before you move into **What *if*,** it is important to capture what you learned in your explorations. The second PMA—the **design criteria**—helps you synthesize important insights and patterns from **What *is*** into a set of criteria you can use to evaluate the concepts you'll generate.

As we've seen, the transition from **What *if*** to **What *wows*** can be jarring: You need to make some tough choices. The third PMA, the **napkin pitch**, helps by laying out the elements of your most promising concepts.

Finally, once you have identified the key assumptions and developed some prototypes to put in front of actual customers, you're ready for a learning launch. Investment in the project will be at its highest point yet—and so will excitement and anxiety, for both the project team and the executive sponsors. The fourth PMA, the **learning guide**, becomes your compass for navigating this exciting final phase. In it you specify what you intend to learn and the financial resources you're willing to commit during your early forays into the marketplace.

On the following pages you will find descriptions of each PMA and templates that can help you manage your own growth projects.

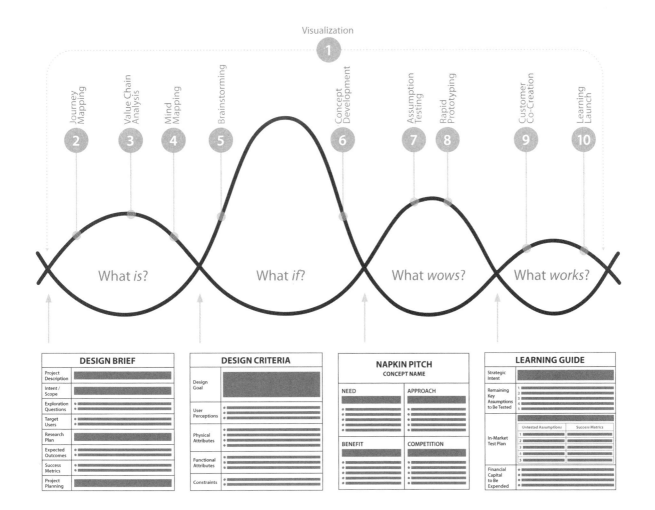

PMA 1: The Design Brief

The design brief will be your North Star throughout a design thinking project, providing a constant answer to the question, "Where are we headed?" A design brief tells the project team where it is going and why, what pitfalls to avoid, and what resources are required. It sets the schedule, names the important milestones, and lays out the metrics that will assess the project.

Not surprisingly, brevity is a key attribute of a good design brief. The document—two or three pages at most—should give the team plenty of leeway to use their creativity. On the classic TV show *Mission Impossible*, each episode opened with what amounts to a design brief. We hope that it will not be necessary for yours to self-destruct—it can come in handy throughout the project.

When to use it: Use the design brief to kick off the project, and revisit it at every key milestone. An experienced designer will not begin work without a brief. If you are leading a team that is asked to start a growth project but receives an incomplete design brief, your first task is to beef it up.

Why the design brief de-risks your growth project: Remember how we said that design thinking is a problem-solving approach that works well for exploring unknown possibilities? Well, explorers often get lost. The immortal Yogi Berra once said, "If you don't know where you're going, you'll probably end up somewhere else." This is an ever-present danger in a design thinking project, and the design brief is your tool for managing that risk. As you map unfamiliar terrain, reframe problems to see opportunities, and imagine alternative futures, you must constantly check your direction (as well as your watch and your gas gauge). The design brief provides that guidance throughout the project.

DESIGN BRIEF

Project Description	What is the business problem or opportunity? Describe the project in a few sentences, as you would in an "elevator pitch."
Intent Scope	What is within the scope of the project and what is outside it? What efforts sit adjacent to this particular project?
Exploration Questions	What key questions will you need to answer through your research? These may include customer needs to understand better, emerging technical possibilities, and new business models.
Target Users	Who are you designing for? Try to be as specific as possible. Whom do you need to understand? Why are they important?
Research Plan	How will you explore your opportunity space? You will need a plan, including a timetable and milestones, for both primary and secondary research.
Expected Outcomes	What outcomes would you like to see?
Success Metrics	How will you measure success?
Project Planning	What resources do you need? Why? At what stages? What is creating the time urgency? What is the relevant time frame for fulfilling the brief?

PMA 2: The Design Criteria

The design criteria PMA is a succinct expression of the ideal end state of your growth project. It captures your conclusions from the **What *is*** stage and provides the yardstick by which possible solutions will be evaluated. Notice that the design criteria do not tell you what to make or how to make it; instead, they describe the attributes of an ideal solution. They are a concise list of relevant constraints and aspirations for the solution. In this, they represent an extension of the design brief, including information you lacked at the start of the process.

When to use it: You develop design criteria at the bridge between **What *is*** and **What *if*.** They are often communicated to the executive sponsor and other stakeholders as an indicator of the progress and direction of the growth project.

Why the design criteria de-risk your growth project: During **What *is*,** you glean new insights from many sources. As a result, growth projects can suffer from information overload. The design criteria distill the incoming data, separate the signal from the noise, and tell you what you truly believe about the ideal solution. Projects that cannot generate concise design criteria become rudderless ships, floating in a sea of data and never arriving at terra firma.

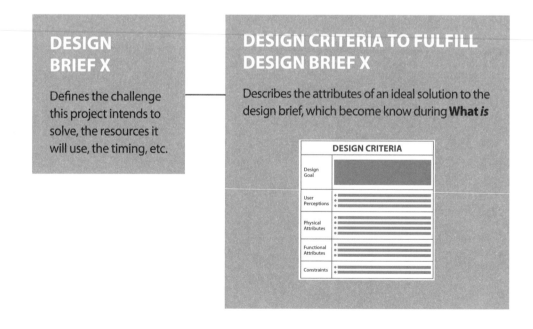

DESIGN BRIEF X

Defines the challenge this project intends to solve, the resources it will use, the timing, etc.

DESIGN CRITERIA TO FULFILL DESIGN BRIEF X

Describes the attributes of an ideal solution to the design brief, which become know during **What *is***

DESIGN CRITERIA

Design Goal	
User Perceptions	
Physical Attributes	
Functional Attributes	
Constraints	

DESIGN CRITERIA

Design Goal	• What have you learned about the target customer? • What needs (functional, emotional, psychological, social) does the design have to fulfill for the target customer? • Why is it strategically important for your organization to address those needs?
User Perceptions	• How important is your proposed offering to the target customer's well-being? • Are there aesthetic attributes necessary to succeed with the target customer? • Does the target customer expect the offering to have certain social, ethical, or ecological attributes? • What does ease-of-use mean to the target customer?
Physical Attributes	• Must the offering be able to capture, store, and /or transmit information about usage? • Does the offering need to be designed for use in specific environments or situations? • Are there weight or size considerations for lifting, use, or transport? • Are there memory, bandwidth, or connectivity issues?
Functional Attributes	• Does the design of the offering need to accommodate specific use-case scenarios? List them in order of importance to the target customer. • Does the design need to address compatibility or standards issues?
Constraints	• Does the final offering need to be completed by a specific date? • What constraints does your current business impose (the offering must use the existing manufacturing base, provide higher profit margins than current offerings, leverage proprietary technologies, etc.)? • Are there ecosystem and regulatory concerns (height of shelves at retailers, OSHA regulations, etc.)?

PMA 3: The Napkin Pitch

The napkin pitch provides a simple, consistent format for summarizing and communicating new concepts. The name derives from the notion that a good idea can be communicated simply, often on the back of a napkin. Because napkins tend to jam printer trays, you translate the concept into a one-page template that may not be useful for wiping your hands but will do a great job of letting you and your team work on multiple growth concepts in parallel.

For a given concept, the napkin pitch describes the target customers, their unmet need, and why your offering creates novel value for them; the elements you will make, buy, and partner for; the channels you will use; and the potential rivals to watch.

When to use it: Use the napkin pitch at the conclusion of concept development, to summarize the short list of concepts coming out of **What *if*** that you want to explore further in the **What *wows*** stage.

Why the napkin pitch de-risks your growth project: Design thinking is about exploring multiple options and letting others validate them. These characteristics introduce a degree of complexity you won't encounter on a more linear project. The napkin pitch enforces simplicity and helps you avoid the temptation to stack the deck before others (especially customers) have an opportunity to validate your thinking. Equally important, it puts concepts into a distilled form that lets collaborators focus on the essential elements as they create prototypes.

NAPKIN PITCH: Concept Name

Need

- What customer wants this?
- What unmet need(s) does it serve?

Approach

- What asset or capability does this leverage?
- How would it create value?
- How will our company create a sustainable advantage?

Benefit

- How will the customer benefit?
- How will our company benefit?
- What other parties will benefit?

Competition

- What firms currently serve this need?
- How will they respond to our entry?

PMA 4: The Learning Guide

The learning guide restates the strategic intent of the project and then defines the parameters for testing the remaining key assumptions. You will use it to address—head on—the nagging fear in the back of everyone's mind: *What if it doesn't work?* It is a great mechanism for defining (a) the overall intent of the new concept, (b) the key assumptions to be tested, (c) the financial resources that will be expended, and (d) the knowledge capital that must be returned, even if the project is not continued.

Corporations have begun using learning guides as a response to a common obstacle to growth: risk aversion. Teams are often inclined to play it safe to avoid a "failure." A learning guide is a form of permission that says, in effect, "As long as you learn more about your key assumptions, your efforts are not a failure."

When to use it: Use the learning guide before you expend resources to engage with customers in formal co-creation sessions. Refresh it before you invest in medium-fidelity prototypes or engage in a learning launch. In fact, any time you spend "real money" (typically five figures) on something that is not a sure thing, it is wise to use a learning guide to inform your investment decisions.

Why the learning guide de-risks your growth project: The success of design thinking depends on your ability to place small bets fast. The learning guide is the mechanism for ensuring that each bet focuses on testing the key assumptions and for keeping the resources of each bet small, so that you can afford to walk away if you don't like the results.

Strategic Intent	Describe in two to three sentences (maximum) what this project is setting out to achieve, both for consumers and for the firm.
Remaining Key Assumptions to Be Tested	List the key assumptions about the concept that you have not yet been able to test with the data you already have. (For more on assumption testing, see Chapter 9.)
In-Market Test Plan	Define which assumptions are most important to answer during this phase. For each one, define what constitutes a successful test by specifying one or more metrics. Here is a good format to use:

Untested Assumptions	Success Metric for Learning Launch
1. (Short description of a key assumption to be tested)	Define how it will be measured and what the threshold for success will be

Financial Capital to Be Expended	Testing these assumptions is deemed to be an acceptable use of the financial resources noted below, even if the results discourage future investment in the growth concept. Describe the capital resources (budget, people) that will be made available during the **What *works*** phase to test key assumptions in the marketplace, whether through co-creation or formal learning launches.

CNVC'S LIST OF UNIVERSAL HUMAN NEEDS

The Center for Nonviolent Communication is a nonprofit organization dedicated to furthering the principles of nonviolence. CNVC assumes that we all share the same basic human needs and that each of our actions helps us meet one or more of those needs. Below is a list of universal needs, provided by CNVC, which provides a great starting point for design thinking projects.

CONNECTION

Acceptance

Affection

Appreciation

Belonging

Cooperation

Communication

Closeness

Community

Companionship

Compassion

Consideration

Consistency

Empathy

Inclusion

Intimacy

Love

Mutuality

Nurturing

Respect/self-respect

Safety

Security

Stability

Support

To know and be known

To see and be seen

To understand and be understood

Trust

Warmth

PHYSICAL WELL-BEING

Air

Food

Movement/exercise

Rest/sleep

Sexual expression

Safety

Shelter

Touch

Water

HONESTY

Authenticity

Integrity

Presence

PLAY
Joy
Humor

PEACE
Beauty
Communion
Ease
Equality
Harmony
Inspiration
Order

AUTONOMY
Choice
Freedom
Independence
Space
Spontaneity

MEANING
Awareness
Celebration of life
Challenge
Clarity
Competence
Consciousness
Contribution

Creativity
Discovery
Efficacy
Effectiveness
Growth
Hope
Learning
Mourning
Participation
Purpose
Self-expression
Stimulation
To matter
Understanding

Website: www.cnvc.org

FURTHER READING

The Art of Innovation: Lessons in Creativity from IDEO, America's Leading Design Firm. Tom Kelley, with Jonathan Littman. Crown Business, 2001

The Back of the Napkin: Solving Problems and Selling Ideas with Pictures. Dan Roam. Portfolio, 2008.

Believe Me: Why Your Vision, Brand, and Leadership Need a Bigger Story. Michael Margolis. Get Storied Press, 2009.

Blink: The Power of Thinking Without Thinking Malcolm Gladwell. Little, Brown, 2005.

"Buchanan's design thinking matrix: implications for SMMEs." Ria (HM) van Zyl. Presented at the International DMI Education Conference "Design Thinking: New Challenges for Designers, Managers and Organizations." 2008

Business Model Generation: A Handbook for Visionaries, Game Changers, and Challengers. Alexander Osterwalder and Yves Pigneur. Wiley, 2010.

Change by Design: How Design Thinking Transforms Organizations and Inspires Innovation. Tim Brown. Harper-Business, 2009.

Creating Breakthrough Products: Innovation from Product Planning to Program Approval. Jonathan Cagan and Craig Vogel. FT Press, 2001.

Design-Driven Innovation: Changing the Rules of Competition by Radically Innovating What Things Mean. Roberto Verganti. Harvard Business Press, 2009.

The Design of Business: Why Design Thinking Is the Next Competitive Advantage. Roger Martin. Harvard Business Press, 2009.

Design Thinking: Integrating Innovation, Customer Experience, and Brand Value. Thomas Lockwood, editor. Allworth Press, 3rd edition, 2009.

Designing Interactions. Bill Moggridge. The MIT Press, 2007.

"The Experience Cycle." Hugh Dubberly and Shelley Evenson. In *Interactions*, 2008.

Experience Design. Nathan Shedroff. Waite Group Press, 2001.

A Fine Line: How Design Strategies Are Shaping the Future of Business. Hartmut Esslinger. Jossey-Bass, 2009.

The Game-Changer: How You Can Drive Revenue and Profit Growth with Innovation. A.G. Lafley and Ram Charan. Crown Business, 2008.

Glimmer: How Design Can Transform Your Life, and Maybe Even the World. Warren Berger. The Penguin Press, 2009.

How Breakthroughs Happen: The Surprising Truth About How Companies Innovate. Andrew Hargadon. Harvard Business School Press, 2003.

Innovation to the Core: A Blueprint for Transforming the Way Your Company Innovates. Peter Skarzynski and Rowan Gibson. Harvard Business School Press, 2008.

Made to Stick: Why Some Ideas Survive and Others Die. Chip Heath and Dan Heath. Random House, 2007.

Making Meaning: How Successful Businesses Deliver Meaningful Customer Experiences. Steve Diller, Nathan Shedroff, and Darrel Rhea. New Riders Press, 2005.

Massive Change. Bruce Mau, Jennifer Leonard, and Institute Without Boundaries. Phaidon Press, 2004.

Open Innovation: The New Imperative for Creating and Profiting from Technology. Henry Chesbrough. Harvard Business School Press, 2003.

The Opposable Mind: Winning Through Integrative Thinking Roger Martin. Harvard Business School Press, 2007.

Positive Turbulence: Developing Climates for Creativity, Innovation, and Renewal. Stanley S. Gryskiewicz. Jossey-Bass, 1999.

"Seizing the White Space: Innovative Service Concepts in the United States." Tim Ogilvie, Jeneanne M. Rae, and Stephen Ezell. Tekes, 2007.

Sketching User Experiences: Getting the Design Right and the Right Design. Bill Buxton. Morgan Kaufmann, 2007.

The Ten Faces of Innovation: IDEO's Strategies for Beating the Devil's Advocate and Driving Creativity Throughout Your Organization. Tom Kelley, with Jonathan Littman. Doubleday, 2005.

Ten Rules for Strategic Innovators: From Idea to Execution. Vijay Govindarajan and Chris Trimble. Harvard Business School Press, 2005.

A Whole New Mind: Why Right-Brainers Will Rule the Future. Daniel H. Pink. Riverhead Books, 2005.

"Wicked Problems in Design Thinking." Richard Buchanan. In *Design Issues*, Vol. 8, no. 2 (1992): 5-21.

Wired to Care: How Companies Prosper When They Create Widespread Empathy. Dev Patnaik, with Peter Mortensen. FT Press, 2009.

NOTES

Section I

1. In Hugh Dubberly, "How Do You Design? A Compendium of Models," March 2005, p. 10. http://www.dubberly.com/wp-content/uploads/2008/06/ddo_designprocess.pdf.

2. Stephen Fry, "The iPad Launch: Can Steve Jobs Do It Again?" *Time*, April 1, 2010. http://www.time.com/time/business/article/0,8599,1976935-3,00.html.

3. See Owen Edwards, *Elegant Solutions* (Three Rivers Press, 1989), pp. 1-8.

4. Richard Buchanan and Victor Margolin (eds.), *Discovering Design: Explorations in Design Studies* (University of Chicago Press, 1995).

5. See, for example, Robert S. Kaplan and David P. Norton, *The Strategy-Focused Organization: How Balanced Scorecard Companies Thrive in the New Business Environment* (Harvard Business School Press, 2000); and Michael C. Mankins and Richard Steele, "Turning Great Strategy into Great Performance," *Harvard Business Review*, July-August 2005.

6. J.N. Wright, "Mission and reality and why not?" *Journal of Change Management*, 3(1): 30-45 (2002).

7. From Duncan's remarks at the Institute for Design Strategy Conference, Chicago, May 2005.

8. See Jeanne Liedtka, Robert Rosen, and Robert Wiltbank, *The Catalyst: How You Can Become an Extraordinary Growth Leader* (Crown Business, 2009).

9. See www.freddieyauner.co.uk.

10. Richard Neustadt and Ernest May, *Thinking in Time: The Uses of History for Decision Makers* (Free Press, 1986).

Section II

1. Lenny T. Mendonca and Hayagreeva Rao, "Lessons from Innovation's Front Lines: An Interview with IDEO's CEO," *McKinsey Quarterly*, November 2008. http://www.mckinseyquarterly.com/Lessons_from_innovations_front_lines_An_interview_with_IDEOs_CEO_2185.

2. In Jonah Lehrer, *How We Decide* (Houghton Mifflin, 2009), p. 196.

3. See Richard Thaler and Cass Sundstein, *Nudge: Improving Decisions About Health, Wealth, and Happiness* (Yale University Press, 2008).

4. In Ellen Langer, *Mindfulness* (Addison Wesley, 1989).

5. Bruno Wicker, Christian Keysers, Jane Plailly, Jean-Pierre Royet, Vittorio Gallese, and Giacomo Rizzolatti, "Both of Us Disgusted in *My* Insula," *Neuron* 40 (3): 655-664, October 2003.

6. Dan Roam, *The Back of the Napkin: Solving Problems and Selling Ideas with Pictures* (Portfolio, 2008), p. 141.

7. Jill Bolte Taylor, *My Stroke of Insight: A Brain Scientist's Personal Journey* (Penguin, 2006), p. 19.

8. See Benson P. Shapiro, V. Kasturi Rangan, and John J. Sviokla, "Staple Yourself to an Order," *Harvard Business Review,* July-August 1992.

Section III

1. Linda Verlee Williams, *Teaching for the Two-Sided Mind* (Simon & Schuster, 1983).

2. Stanley Gryskiewicz, "Trial by Fire in an Industrial Setting: A Practical Evaluation of Three Creative Problem-Solving Techniques," in K. Gronhaug and G. Kaufmann (eds.), *Innovation: A Cross-Disciplinary Perspective* (Oxford University Press, 1988).

Section IV

1. Neustadt and May, *Thinking in Time*, p. 251.

Section V

1. In Rob Koplowitz, "How Social Technologies Can Kickstart Innovation," CIO, September 16, 2010. http://www.cio.com/article/615114/How_Social_Technologies_Can_Kickstart_Innovation.

2. In Patricia Seybold, *Outside Innovation: How Your Customers Will Co-Design Your Company's Future* (Collins, 2006).

Section VI

1. Jessie Scanlon, "LifeTuner: How AARP Came to Serve Twentysomethings," *BusinessWeek,* November 11, 2009. http://www.businessweek.com/innovate/content/nov2009/id20091110_992142.htm

2. See Liedtka, Rosen, and Wiltbank, *The Catalyst*.

ABOUT THE AUTHORS

Jeanne Liedtka

Jeanne Liedtka is a member of the Strategy, Ethics, and Entrepreneurship area at the University of Virginia's Darden School of Business, where she has taught since 1989. Formerly the executive director of the school's Batten Institute, a foundation established to develop thought leadership in the fields of entrepreneurship and innovation, Jeanne has also served as chief learning officer for the United Technologies Corporation (UTC), headquartered in Hartford, Connecticut, and as the associate dean of the MBA program at Darden. Jeanne's current teaching responsibilities focus on design thinking, innovation, and organic growth in Darden's MBA and Executive Education programs.

Jeanne's current research explores how design thinking can be used to enrich our ability to create inclusive strategic conversations about organizational futures. Her previous book, *The Catalyst: How You Can Become an Extraordinary Growth Leader* (Crown Business, 2009), is based on a three-year Batten Institute study of operating managers who excelled at producing revenue growth in mature organizations. *The Catalyst,* coauthored by Robert Rosen and Robert Wiltbank, was named by *BusinessWeek* as one of the best innovation and design books of 2009.

Jeanne received her DBA in Management Policy from Boston University and her MBA from the Harvard Business School. She has been involved in the corporate strategy field since beginning her career as a strategy consultant for the Boston Consulting Group.

Tim Ogilvie

Tim Ogilvie is the CEO of Peer Insight, an innovation strategy consultancy, where he has made pioneering contributions to the emerging disciplines of service innovation, customer experience design, and business model exploration. His clients include AARP, Bank of America, Diebold, GE, Hallmark, Hewlett-Packard, Pfizer, Procter & Gamble, Starwood Hotels, and The Hartford. His projects seek to create organic growth by using design thinking methods to link new customer experiences to scalable business models.

He has also consulted to five governments and influenced innovation policy from the United States to the European Union to Taiwan. In 2007 he coauthored "Seizing the White Space: Innovative Service Concepts in the United States," published by Tekes, the Finnish funding agency for R&D. This publication established the precepts for service innovation that are being embraced by public policy makers and leading private firms in the European Union.

Tim is a visiting lecturer at the University of Virginia's Darden School of Business, where he teaches customer-centered design and innovation. He holds a master's degree in Computer Integrated Manufacturing Systems from the Georgia Institute of Technology and a BA in English from the University of Virginia.